That's How I Found Her

That's How I Found Her

My Grandfather's Holocaust Journey

Jessica Kaplan

URIM PUBLICATIONS

Jerusalem · New York

That's How I Found Her
My Grandfather's Holocaust Journey
by Jessica Kaplan

Typeset by Juliet Tresgallo

Printed in the USA
First Edition
ISBN 978-965-524-379-6

Urim Publications
P.O. Box 52287
Jerusalem 9152102
Israel

www.UrimPublications.com

Library of Congress Cataloging-in-Publication Data in progress.

PREFACE

A GAINST ALL ODDS, Kalman Steuer (born Sztajer) and his wife Genia survived the Holocaust and immigrated to the United States in May, 1946. They rebuilt their lives, first settling on the Lower East Side of Manhattan and then in Danielson, Connecticut, where they operated a chicken farm and were among the founders of Temple Beth Israel. After the tragic death of their son in 1962, they persevered. With resolve and faith, the Steuers again overcame adversity, raising their daughter and eventually helping to raise their three grandchildren.

This book is Kalman's story – of willpower, survival, and hope.

CHAPTER 1

I T WAS BEFORE we knew to close the shutters. The three of us stood in front of our second-floor window and looked out onto the street. We watched. We stared. If the German soldiers had glanced up, they would have seen three faces peering down in shock, three heads, all the same shape, with the same deep brown hair. They would have seen three pairs of chestnut brown eyes, one pair slightly larger than the other two, fixated on the scene below.

Our parents had already left for work, and we were sitting at the table finishing up breakfast when the commotion began. We jumped up from the table and ran to the window as soon as we heard the noise. Two jeeps screeched to a halt, boots crushed the gravel street below, and men yelled in German I did not understand. We heard one German soldier bark orders as others dragged Chaim Greenbaum, along with his older brother and his father, out of the apartment building directly across the street from our own. The Greenbaum men squatted, their arms unbent in front of them, elbows locked, palms facing the ground, when we heard Mr. Greenbaum's desperate voice through the open window.

"Please, please," he begged, "leave my boys. They haven't done anything. It was me. I was the only one."

Chaim and his brother crouched in their socks, shoeless, their shirts untucked as though they did not have time to finish getting dressed before they were hauled outside. The brothers held their heads up high, trembling silently. I could not see their faces clearly. I am glad I did not see their eyes. Their father sobbed as he pleaded for his sons to be spared.

Then, after three short pops, silence. The soldiers, in their stiff uniforms and polished boots, did not say a word as the tallest among them shot each of the Greenbaum men in the back of the head. We watched them fall forward in quick succession. Chaim fell last. And when it was all over, two young German soldiers tossed the bodies of our neighbors into the back of an open jeep and drove off.

"Kalman?" Herschel whispered.

I tore my eyes from the shocking scene and pulled the shutters closed. I turned the brass latch, locking out, at least temporarily, the world outside. The boys had seen enough. Aaron's shoulders began to quiver. The tears were coming. Not just Aaron's tears – mine too. But I willed myself not to cry as I closed my eyes and remembered Chaim Greenbaum.

Chaim and I had been classmates since Heder.[1] Chaim grew into a tall skinny teenager with arms so long that the sleeves of his sweater never reached his wrists. They must have been cold in the winter. His mother always packed an extra sandwich for lunch. My mother did the same. Every day, she would hand me two small sacks as I headed out the door to school. One for me, and an identical one with a sandwich for another boy in my class. All of the mothers who had enough to spare sent an extra lunch. As class president, it was my job to collect the extra lunch sacks in the morning, and at lunchtime, I handed a sack to each boy who did not bring his own lunch to school. No student went hungry at a Jewish school in Sosnowiec. It was our community's way of helping the needy.

"Kalman?"

This time it was Aaron whispering my name.

I looked down at him and saw a steady stream of tears. Reminiscing about my childhood would have to wait. I put one arm around each of my brothers. Herschel's shoulders were stiff. He was trying so hard to be brave. Aaron was trembling, clearly terrified. I wish I could have told them that everything would be okay. I wish I could have told them that when our parents returned from work, we would all go back to the house in the country where we had spent the summer. I wish

---

1. Heder, literally "room," was a widespread form of Jewish elementary education in pre-war Eastern Europe.

I could have told them that we would forget about the Greenbaum brothers and the Nazis. The truth is, I could not, in good conscience, tell them any of those things. I had no idea whether anything would ever return to the way it was before the fall of 1939.

"Herschel, Aaron," I finally said. "It's time for school."

It was September 1939, and school still provided the boys some sense of normalcy in a world that was anything but normal.

"But Kalman, is it safe to go outside?" Aaron asked, backing away from the window.

I nodded and looked through the thin slats of the shutters as I sent the boys to get their coats. It looked ordinary outside, so ordinary that I wondered if I had just imagined the whole scene. I could not have just watched Chaim Greenbaum murdered. Impossible. I felt a chill. A draft had come through that window for as long as I remembered but it seemed so much colder that day.

I grabbed my coat off the hook as I followed my brothers out the door.

"We will be fine. I'll walk you to school this morning," I told them.

The boys usually walked to school themselves, but they needed me with them today. Or maybe it was I who needed them. My uncle wouldn't mind if I were late to the factory.

I was eighteen, Herschel was eleven and Aaron was nine. We were the three sons of Nachum and Leah Sztajer. Our older sister, Julia, and our parents had left for work shortly before we heard the jeeps skidding to a stop in the street.

We walked out of our apartment and down the stairs in silence. I felt Aaron's small hand grab mine as we left our building.

"What have you learned about the Torah portion this week?" I asked, attempting to distract my brothers.

Neither boy answered. Herschel stared at the entrance to the Greenbaum's building. Aaron looked down and squeezed my hand. I squeezed back.

"Let's walk quickly, it's windy," I said as I turned in the direction of the boys' school.

Maybe if I had stopped to look closely, I would have seen remnants of blood on the ground where the Greenbaums were shot, but I could not bear to glance in that direction. I looked straight ahead and hoped my brothers did too. I thought about telling them not to look, but I knew that as soon as I would say, "don't look at that spot," two heads would turn in exactly that direction. It would be like placing the boys on the edge of a rooftop and telling them not to look down. I did not want to remind the boys of that morning's events. It was the first time we saw death at the hands of the Nazis, and we had seen enough.

As we passed the bakery and I inhaled the smell of fresh bread, I felt like I just woke up from a weird dream. Everything else seemed too ordinary. The bakery had its daily line snaking around the corner. The usual group of young Hasidim stood outside the Rodomsker Yeshiva down the street. The streets were full of children on their way to school. It looked like a typical morning in Sosnowiec.

I thought I knew Chaim Greenbaum, but maybe I did not. One never knows what happens behind closed doors. Maybe he and his family did something terrible. Is it possible? Did I really just watch innocent men shot down in the street? There must have been a reason, I thought. Mr. Greenbaum had said it was all him, that his sons had nothing to do with whatever it was he had done. Maybe he had done something, I told myself repeatedly as I walked. But no matter how many times I heard my voice inside my head, I could not believe that the Greenbaums deserved their fate.

The boys stopped suddenly. Lost in thought, I did not realize that we had arrived in front of their school. I bent at my knees so that I was at eye level with my brothers.

"Kalman, will you pick us up after school today?" Aaron asked as both boys looked at me.

Before I had a chance to answer, Herschel did.

"The two of us will walk home together Aaron, as usual."

Herschel spoke loudly and clearly. His voice sounded older. But he wasn't looking at Aaron when he spoke to him. He was staring at me, his eyes pleading. I could not tell if he was asking me to let him be brave, to show me that he was strong enough to be responsible for his little brother on the walk home that day. Or was he asking me to save him from taking on that responsibility? Did he want me to say no, I would not allow them to walk home alone? Did he want me to insist that I would pick them up after school?

"I will be waiting right here when school ends," I said.

Aaron smiled but Herschel did not react. I still could not figure out what he wanted. I wanted to protect them, but that is not why I said I would pick them up from school. When I got to the factory, my uncle would ask why I was late to work. I would have to tell him about the Greenbaums. He would insist that I leave work early to meet the boys after school, and he would even give me a few zlote to buy them each a small treat on the way home.

CHAPTER 2

L IFE WAS CHANGING quickly. It was not even a week ago that I was woken shortly after five o'clock in the morning by the sound of anti-aircraft fire. I had jumped out of bed when the blasts began and found my parents and Julia standing in the kitchen.

"What is that sound?" I asked.

It sounded like a constant stream of thunder interrupted every few seconds by a deafening bang. By some miracle, Aaron and Herschel slept through the cacophony.

"Anti-aircraft fire," said my father, rubbing his eyes.

"Against the Germans? Already?" I asked no one in particular.

We knew war was coming. Everyone knew war was coming. The Polish government had been preparing for months, amassing troops along the German border, and strategizing with Britain and France about how best to defend Poland from the German invasion. But I could not believe it was actually here. Would Poland survive a war with Germany? Would my family survive a war with Germany?

"What will we do?" my mother asked, with all of my questions and fears wrapped up in the look of terror in her eyes.

"For now, we will do nothing," my father told her. "Until we hear it is safe, we will stay inside. Together. And when the boys wake up, we will do our best to act normal and shield them from this war for as long as possible."

So that is what I did. I tried to act like it was just another Friday, not just for the boys, but for my mother too, and honestly, for myself. But it wasn't so much acting normal as it was acting like someone else entirely. I spent that first day of the war impersonating a young man with the strength and confidence to face the future as his world falls apart.

When the anti-aircraft fire finally died down, we heard only silence. Julia, Herschel, Aaron, and I spent the day playing cards and reading. My mother prepared for Shabbat,[2] and my father sat in the kitchen and listened to the radio all day, hoping to learn something about the German advance. When he shut the radio before sundown, he still had no information about the war or our safety.

It was the first time in my eighteen years that I remember spending Shabbat without visiting friends and family. Every Shabbat since I was a little boy, I walked straight from Synagogue to my grandfather's apartment where he tested me on the weekly Torah portion. My grandfather passed away in 1935, but I still visited my grandmother after attending services each week, along with my aunts, uncles, and cousins. And of course, I missed Friday night at Promenade Street, where all the teenagers socialized after dinner. The Poles always stayed on one side of the street and the Jews on the other, but aside from some dirty looks, we did not bother each other.

Without those activities, Saturday was quiet and lonely. Antsy to hear the news, I turned on the radio as soon as Shabbat ended. According to German radio, German troops had not yet entered Poland, but it would not be long before German soldiers marched into Sosnowiec. No one knew when food deliveries would follow. Early the next morning, my parents took my brothers to buy food and essentials. They told us that stores were full of people who anxiously bought whatever they could, arguing with each other and the shopkeepers over the few available goods. All of the groceries in town were bought in just a few hours, as shipments of goods were delayed, and everyone wanted to stock up before the German troops arrived.

Julia and I started the day by walking over to the Ecksteins' apartment. Yitzchak and Shprinza Eckstein lived in a large apartment

---

2. Shabbat, the Jewish Sabbath, commemorates the seventh day on which God rested after creation. It is observed from shortly before sunset on Friday evening until three stars appear in the sky on Saturday night. For observant Jews like Kalman, it is a day of joy, during which one refrains from work and instead spends the day eating traditional meals, praying, studying, and spending time with family and friends.

in the center of town. My own parents were comfortable financially, but the Ecksteins were considered wealthy by Sosnowiec standards. Yitzchak was a successful businessman and a leader in the Jewish community.

The Ecksteins had three sons, Sol, Henry, and Max, and a daughter named Genia. Max and Julia had been dating for the past year, and Genia was my childhood sweetheart. I had known her my whole life and I remember the day that I first asked her to be my girlfriend. She was only twelve at the time, and I was fifteen. We were leaving a meeting of Hanoar Hatzioni, a Zionist youth movement in which we were active at the time. We were all dressed up in our Zionist scout uniforms, and I couldn't take my eyes off her as we walked down the street. I summoned the courage to ask her to be my girlfriend as we walked, and she looked down at her shoes.

"I have to ask my mother. I'll let you know tomorrow."

The next day she told me that her mother said no, but I was persistent, and her mother must have said yes at some point because while I do not remember exactly when, I cannot remember a time we were not together. I could not wait to see her after these last few days of uncertainty. We lived just a few blocks apart, but her life was different than mine in many ways. Her family ate on fine china. They slept on embroidered monogrammed sheets and employed a Polish housekeeper who did all the cleaning and cooking in their home. Genia's parents and brothers spoiled her completely. She had her brothers wrapped around her little finger, especially Sol. Ten years her senior, Sol could not bear for her to be the least bit unhappy, so on the rare occasions that her parents said no to one of her requests, Sol stepped in.

Genia was also very smart. She planned to go to university when she graduated from high school. Maybe even medical school. I knew she loved me as I loved her and was probably waiting for me to come see her this morning.

It seemed like the entire population of Sosnowiec was outside, the noise amplified. Maybe it was because I was used to the quiet after being inside for so long, or maybe the people really were that loud. Children had been confined indoors for days and were shrieking as they ran around playing with friends. As we neared the Ecksteins' building, I broke into a run and Julia could not keep up.

"Kalman, slow down," she screamed as I ran into a small woman carrying a bin of trash. It was the Ecksteins' housekeeper, Wanda. She looked at me as the bin fell and the trash spilled out onto the street.

"I'm sorry Wanda, I am just so excited to be out of the house and on my way to see Genia," I said as I bent down to help her pick up the trash and put it back in the bin.

"If you hadn't been running."

Julia must have caught up. Always the big sister. She was out of breath, standing next to me and rolling her eyes.

"It's okay sweetie," Wanda said. "You go inside. Genia will be happy to see you. I will clean up this mess. I have plenty of time. Mr. Eckstein told me to leave for the day right after I take out this trash."

"But the day has just begun," I said, surprised.

I wondered why Mr. Eckstein told Wanda to leave early. He was a demanding boss who normally insisted that their home be spotless and an elaborate dinner prepared daily.

"Genia, Max," I yelled as I bounded up the stone staircase to the third floor.

"Kalman," I heard as the door opened. Mr. Eckstein stood in the entry.

"Good morning, Kalman," he said.

"Good morning, Mr. Eckstein."

"How is your family holding up, Kalman? Is that Julia behind you?"

Julia reached the top of the stairs, breathless. I must have been running quickly.

"Good morning, Mr. Eckstein," she said. "It has been a long few days. It feels so good to get outside. Our parents took Herschel and Aaron to buy groceries and Kalman and I came straight over here."

"Come join me in the kitchen, children."

My parents also called us children. Julia was twenty! I wondered at what point we would stop being children in the eyes of our parents' generation. Surely, if Mr. Eckstein had known then how soon we would grow up, he would have used a different word.

We walked into the kitchen. Genia and her mother both stood up to greet us. No one spoke as we all hugged. I held onto Genia a little longer than I normally would have with her parents in the room.

"The boys are out. They went to see about joining the Air Attack Patrol. It's a group of volunteers who are going to keep watch for German airplanes. It's organized by Sergeant Sadorovich, the hero from the last war. As of this morning, he's accepting Jewish volunteers too." Genia said. "Would you like some tea while we wait for them?"

"Yes, please," we responded in unison and Genia filled the tea pot with water.

The rest of us sat down. Mr. Eckstein's leg shook underneath the table as he told us what he knew about the German advance. Hitler's plans to invade Poland had moved a step closer to fruition at the end of August, when the Germans and Soviets signed the Molotov-Ribbentrop Pact. A non-aggression pact in which Germany and the Soviet Union agreed not to attack each other, the agreement removed the threat of Soviet opposition to a German invasion of Poland, increasing the likelihood of German success.

Mr. Eckstein told us about a recent clash between German and Polish troops. On the evening of August 31, 1939, a team of German operatives disguised themselves as Polish insurgents and stormed a radio station transmitter in the German border town of Gleiwitz. They pushed their way into the station, got a hold of a microphone, and broadcast a brief anti-German message. News of the incident spread within hours, with Germany reporting that its transmitter had been hijacked by Polish insurgents. Germany had manufactured a pretext for the following day's offensive.

The start of that offensive is what we heard the previous Friday, September 1, when we woke up to anti-aircraft fire. The German air force was better equipped than its Polish counterpart, and the Polish army was not adequately prepared to fight the invasion. The cavalry would be no match for the German war machine.

Mr. Eckstein continued to talk about the war as the kettle whistled and I stood to pour water into our teacups. He was hopeful that Great Britain and France would stick to the commitments they made after the invasion of Czechoslovakia to defend Poland in the event of a German invasion – especially the stronger Great Britain. After the signing of the Molotov-Ribbentrop Pact, Great Britain and

Poland signed an Agreement of Mutual Assistance, guaranteeing mutual military assistance if a European country attacked either of them. Military assistance from Great Britain would quickly send the Germans packing. Mr. Eckstein said that if Great Britain had not just recently signed the agreement, Sosnowiec's streets would already be full of German soldiers.

"Let's see if anything new has happened," Mr. Eckstein said as he turned on the radio, and we heard the now familiar roar of Hitler's voice spewing hatred over the airwaves. His speeches had been broadcast constantly over the last few days, as Germany now controlled our airwaves, like it would the skies above.

Mrs. Eckstein turned the knob. I had never seen her looking so angry. Her face red, her eyes filled with hatred of their own, she turned and turned and turned the dial. Her thin fingers moved so quickly. Our options were Hitler or Wagner. There was no news report on the radio.

Julia stood up.

"We should head home," she said. "I don't think we should wait for Max."

She was probably uncomfortable with Mrs. Eckstein's demeanor, as was I. But she was right that it was time to leave. Our parents had their hands full, and we were needed at home. I rose to join her as Genia grabbed my hand.

"I will come back as soon as everything is settled at home," I told her.

"And I will tell Max to come over to your apartment when my brothers get home," Genia added.

Julia and I let ourselves out and walked down the stairs and into the street. People were everywhere. Everyone seemed to be carrying something. Bags from the grocer, sacks of potatoes, and meat from the butcher. One mother pushed a baby carriage right past us. What if she needed clean diapers or baby food while she was cooped up at home with a baby? It made me think about all the people already struggling before this war had really begun, people whose needs were far greater than mine.

Children continued to run wild through the streets, as though it were a holiday. We walked home past countless soccer balls flying and sword fights with sticks. We passed the yeshiva, the bakery, the butcher shop, the Great Synagogue,[3] and all the other familiar sights in town.

As we turned the corner onto our street, we saw Herschel standing in front of our building.

"Daddy wants us all to go to the Ecksteins' apartment," he said.

"We were just there," I responded as we walked past him toward the stairs.

"He says it's safer there," Herschel yelled after us as he followed us up to our apartment.

Our parents must have heard us on the stairs because they immediately met us at the door. I saw two overnight bags sitting on the bench next to the coat rack, and my father spoke.

"We went shopping right after you left for the Ecksteins' this morning. Thank God we were able to buy enough food to tide us over for a short while. The boys had a chance to run around with their friends, and we were able to check on your Bubbe.[4] We even ran into Max and his brothers. They have joined the Air Attack Patrol. Everyone seems to be doing alright under the circumstances. I am concerned, though, of what will happen when the German soldiers come into town. Our building is very close to the edge of town, and I worry that it will be one of the first buildings the soldiers see on their way. Rumor has it that they will arrive sometime in the next day or two and it will be more dangerous at our home. Max suggested that we stay at the Ecksteins for a few days because it will be safer in the center of town. I agree."

He continued to tell us the plan. Our mother would prepare food to bring over to the Ecksteins' home. Our parents had already packed the small bags of clothing by the door for them and the boys. Julia and I were to pack a few things to bring with us. Then, my father and I would secure all the windows, and we would walk over to the Ecksteins together.

---

3. The Great Synagogue was the largest synagogue in Sosnowiec. It was built in 1896 and located on Dekerta Street.

4. "Bubbe" is the Yiddish word for grandmother.

As he finished speaking, we heard banging at the door. It was my cousin.

"My mother sent me," he said, breathless after what I assumed was a sprint from his home a few blocks away all the way up the stairs to our apartment.

"We are going to head out of town to get ahead of the Germans," he continued. "My father is filling up his truck with gasoline, and then we will drive around town to pick up the whole family. Be ready to leave late this afternoon."

He turned and ran down the stairs before any of us had a chance to respond.

Most of my extended family lived in Sosnowiec. My mother's eldest brother owned a roofing business and had a small factory just outside town, where he produced roofing parts. I had been working at the factory for the last few months and often drove his truck to worksites. It was a standard size pickup truck, so I wondered how it would possibly fit the whole family.

"We won't all fit," I told my father.

"We will fit," he said firmly. "We are leaving town with your uncle and the rest of the family. Your Bubbe will have her entire family with her during this difficult time. We will figure out a way to make it work for her sake."

All parents have that single unmistakable tone of voice their children know means business, the one they use when there is no use questioning or arguing. I heard my father speak and I recognized his. I would do as I was told.

I also knew that he thought I did not want to join the rest of the family because I was hesitant to leave without Genia. He was partially right. I was not happy at the prospect of leaving Sosnowiec without Genia, and I was sure that Julia felt the same way about leaving without Max. But I truly could not imagine how all my aunts, uncles, and cousins would fit in that truck.

"Go pack your things," my father said.

I turned, took an empty bag from the cabinet, and walked past the kitchen where I saw my mother standing over the stove. She lifted her head to look at me as I passed, and I saw her eyes full of tears. I felt her eyes follow me as I walked, but I did not turn around. I could not let her see the tears forming in my own.

When I finished packing my bag, my father and I boarded up the windows in anticipation of the upcoming invasion. I was surprised to see that my father had enough wood boards to protect our windows and even some left over that we used for the windows of the Cohens, an elderly couple who lived downstairs and had gone to stay with their daughter and her family just outside the city. Last week, their son-in-law came to pick them up with a horse and buggy, and as they left, my mother promised that we would watch over their apartment. My father must have been planning for this day. We finished with their windows and then returned home, to the smell of sauteed onions.

As I had expected, my uncle arrived several hours later with his truck overflowing with relatives. We walked down the stairs at the sound of the honk, and we saw literally all our relatives on my mother's side of the family sitting on top of suitcases in the cargo bed. My father jogged over to the driver's side of the truck and had a short conversation with my uncle. Then, my uncle got out of the truck, hugged my father, got back in the truck, and drove away. Cousins, aunts, and uncles waved at us as they rode out of town. I watched my father, his head down, slowly walk back across the street to where the rest of us were standing. Our overnight bags were at our feet, and Julia and I each held a pot. I kept my eyes fixed on my father as I inhaled the scent emanating from the pot in my hands. The familiar smell of my mother's stew provided some comfort in that moment. For the second time that day, I could not turn to look at my mother, standing next to me. I heard her quietly sobbing as she watched her own mother, brothers, nieces, and nephews drive away. Her only sister had moved to New York City several years earlier.

"We will stay with the Ecksteins," my father said. "Your uncle said the family would stay away from the city for a few days and return when things settle down here. I insisted that they go on without us. I do not know how that truck is still moving with so much weight on it, and we are six more people. If we get on, we will most definitely overload it. I do not want us to be the reason no one in this family gets out of town today."

He turned around and began to walk briskly toward the center of town. My mother raced to catch up, and they led us, silently, as I walked through the streets of town for the third time that day. It was as if our parents were leading a small march, our family walking two-by-two, with my brothers following my parents and Julia and me bringing up the rear, a small procession away from our home. And sadly, the first of too many marches in which I would participate over the next few years.

CHAPTER 3

IN JUST A few hours, the streets of Sosnowiec had turned from ordinary to desolate. As the sun set, the children disappeared from the streets. Stores were closed, their windows and doors boarded up, and the city was eerily quiet. Silent.

We arrived at the Ecksteins' building just before dark, and as we climbed the stairs, Sol and Henry raced down past us. They were on their way to serve their first shift in the Air Attack Patrol.

"Stay safe," my father said as they passed.

"We will do our best," Henry answered, with none of his usual swagger.

Henry was the wild one in the Eckstein family. Genia's brothers were all strong and tough, the kind of guys who would have scared me if I did not know them so well. But Henry was really bold and sometimes scary, tough as nails. A true wild child, Henry had been kicked out of the Jewish school in Sosnowiec and finished high school at the local Polish school. A lone Jew in Polish public school had to be fearless, even reckless – Henry was both. That day was the first time I heard his voice betray the slightest bit of uncertainty.

Genia opened the door as we approached, and Julia and I headed straight to the kitchen where we put our pots on the hot stove. The dining-room table was set with china as always, and after we all washed up, we sat down to dinner. My mother had cooked plenty of food for all of us, and Mrs. Eckstein put the food she had prepared aside, to be saved for later. We assumed the Germans would be invading shortly and did not know when the next time was that we would be able to go out and restock.

Dinner was enlightening. I saw clearly, for the first time, the vast gap in how my generation and that of my parents viewed Germany. Mr. Eckstein, the most educated man at the table, was adamant that the Germans were a civilized people and that as long as we followed their guidelines, we had nothing to fear. The Ecksteins were both German and had moved their family to Sosnowiec when Genia was a toddler. Max banged furiously on the table with a rolled-up magazine as he argued with his father. He spread open the magazine to show us photographs of synagogues burning in Germany. Mr. and Mrs. Eckstein, and my parents too, would not hear of the possibility that the Germans would burn our synagogues. A heated discussion about what the Germans were or were not capable of went on for a couple of hours, until it was time for all of us to go to sleep.

It seemed to me like I was awake all night watching my brothers sleep on the floor next to me, waiting for something to happen. I must have fallen asleep at some point, because I was woken by Sol and Henry coming home as the sun began to rise. They went straight to the table where they eagerly finished the leftovers from last night's dinner. I stretched as I got up to join them at the table and hear about their patrol.

"Any news?" I asked.

"Sergeant Sadorovich says it won't be long before we see German tanks in the streets," Sol answered.

We all knew Sergeant Sadorovich. He was a Polish hero from the last war who lived in Sosnowiec. He organized the air raid patrols, but he knew as well as anyone else that there was no way for the German army to be stopped. It was just a question of time.

The rest of mine and Genia's families began to rise, and we spent the morning sitting around nervously drinking tea. There was nothing to do. We were afraid to go outside. Herschel and Aaron were the only ones who ate. The rest of us were too nervous. There was one radio station playing Polish folk music, and we listened to that until it turned into static.

Finally, sometime in the afternoon, we heard tanks. The sound was paralyzing. We were completely still, as if our lives depended on a children's game of freeze-dance. I sat in a chair at the dining table without moving or speaking. I felt like I was standing in a library with my head stuck inside an engine. Silent yet so loud. The only sound coming from inside was the ticking of the ornate grandfather clock sitting in the apartment foyer. Finally, Mr. Eckstein stood.

"Sit down Yitzchak," his wife said sharply. "They may see you standing in the window." She whispered, but it was a stern sounding whisper that would have been a yell if she were not so afraid to make a sound.

Mrs. Eckstein was probably right. The Ecksteins had boarded up most of their windows, but the smaller ones were left uncovered, and we were able to see outside through those; that meant the Germans would be able to see through them too. Mr. Eckstein ignored his wife as he tiptoed over to the clock, opened a small wooden door, stuck his left hand inside, and closed the door. Now it was truly silent. The clock was stuck at 2:17 PM.

Henry stood.

"Let's all put our shoes on," he said, rather loudly.

"Quiet Henry," his mother whispered in that same would-have-yelled-if-she-could-have-yelled kind of whisper.

"Why? They can't hear us, their tanks are so noisy, they likely cannot even hear themselves think."

Henry was right. Surely the Germans couldn't hear us. Fear had made us silent.

"Put on your shoes just in case," Henry continued.

"In case of what?" Aaron asked as he climbed onto my father's lap.

His little boy voice reminded me that he was only nine years old; he should not have to suffer through a war, I thought.

No one answered Aaron's question. None of us knew what we were preparing for or how to plan for the unknown. We continued to listen to the tanks and then the jeeps drive by for what felt like days, but probably was no more than an hour or two. Soon after, the rumbling was joined by soldiers yelling in German. I understood only a few words of German. The Ecksteins sometimes spoke German in their home, and I had picked up a few words over the years. Then we heard a few bursts of what I assumed was gunfire, as Henry yelled "get away from the windows!" and we hurried to sit on the floor.

It felt so hot inside the apartment. It was still early September, and with so many windows boarded up, we were sweating. Through the unboarded windows, we could see the sun shining. It was a summery day, one that I would have thought beautiful under other circumstances. I found myself thinking that the German soldiers must have been very hot inside their tanks, likely sweating buckets. It made me feel a bit better for just a split second, to think that they were suffering in any way.

And then, the shouting began.

"Get out Jews! Out! Out!" The soldiers yelled in German.

"Quickly, quickly exit your homes and enter the street! Jews! Jews!"

I knew enough German to understand what we were being told. But Genia's brothers did not want to go. They were not accustomed to recognizing authority or obeying rules.

"We're not going out there," Sol said as he rose and walked over to the door, crossing his arms in front of him.

Max and Henry stood and joined their brother – they were a formidable trio, a wall of muscle, effectively blocking any of us from leaving.

"Boys," Mr. Eckstein said, "we do not have a choice. We must go."

"There is always a choice, father." Now it was Max's turn to speak up.

"In the kitchen, now," Mr. Eckstein said in his wife's would-have-yelled-if-he-could-have-yelled tone. He looked back and forth between his sons and my little brothers as he spoke.

The Eckstein brothers reluctantly followed their father into the kitchen. I appreciated Mr. Eckstein's concern for my brothers, as they did not need to witness more conflict in the face of recent events. Nor did they need to know how afraid the rest of us were of what awaited us in the street (or inside if we refused to go out).

I waited nervously while the Eckstein men whispered, listening to the chaos in the stairwell as the building's other inhabitants made their way downstairs and outside. I could not decipher the hushed conversation in the Ecksteins' kitchen, but the four of them joined us at the door just a few minutes later. It seemed that Mr. Eckstein won. I was not surprised. Despite their rebellious natures, the Eckstein brothers usually listened to their father – only their father. Mr. Eckstein left the apartment first, followed by his sons, then Genia and Mrs. Eckstein. My family walked behind them, my father and I bringing up the rear, as Aaron held my mother's hand in front of us.

We were among the last inhabitants of the building to arrive downstairs. We joined the mass of people already in the street, and in the commotion, Sol grabbed my arm.

"Follow me," he said, "and bring your father with you."

I looked at him in shock.

"They will hurt the men first. My father knows the plan. He will join us too."

Now I knew what the kitchen discussion was really about. I took my father's arm and quickly followed Sol and the other Eckstein men around the corner, back into the side door of their building. We climbed up the back stairwell with our heads down, ignoring the tumult of the street, and walked directly to the apartment. Once inside, we all sat on the floor. None of us spoke or stood to look out the window. I thought about Aaron's small hand clutching my mother's, and wondered if my father had told my mother, Julia, or the boys where we would be. Did they think we just abandoned them in the street? Or worse, that something terrible had happened to us?

After a couple of hours, the women and my brothers returned to the apartment. They had spent those hours just standing around in the street, waiting for something to happen. Nothing did. The German soldiers ignored them until it was announced that all of the women and children were permitted to return home. Julia said she saw some men dragged away in the commotion, but thankfully the boys and our mothers seemed to have missed that development.

The women and children had not been worried about us; they knew where we were. Max had told Julia as they walked down the stairs that the men planned to return to the apartment. Those guys were even bolder than I had thought.

After the drama of that day, my parents decided it was best for my brothers to return to the familiarity of home. Just before dark, the six of us walked again through deserted streets until we reached our building. I was afraid to be outside but acted as though it was completely normal for there to be Germans in uniform in Sosnowiec. Maybe, I thought, if I pretended to be brave, a little bit of that courage may become real. A handful of German jeeps were parked throughout the city, and we walked past a few German soldiers, but none of them bothered, or even acknowledged, us. Maybe things would be okay under German occupation.

But the next morning, I changed my mind. We had barely woken up when a neighbor knocked on our door in tears and told us that her husband was taken by the newly arrived Germans. The Eckstein brothers were right; the Germans did take some of the men. A couple of hundred Jewish men were dragged from the streets outside their homes to City Hall, where they were packed into the basement with hardly any room to breathe. They were held there, under guard, with no food or water, and no sanitary facilities, where they were beaten. The religious men suffered further as the Germans pulled their beards off their faces. After about twenty-four hours, the men were all released.

That was the beginning of our terror under the Nazis.

CHAPTER 4

THE FOLLOWING WEEK, just a couple of days after we witnessed the Greenbaums' murder, the Nazis burned down the Great Synagogue. Wehrmacht[5] soldiers stood guard outside. They did not allow anyone in or out of the building. The few people inside perished while a crowd of Jews gathered outside watching the flames. The Torahs, prayer books, and furniture were destroyed. Synagogues in nearby cities of Bedzin and Katowice were also burned that day. The next morning, Jews were grabbed off the street and forced to clean up the ruins. Some people clearing the rubble took bricks home with them, small mementos of a quickly vanishing world.

Disorganization followed. We later learned that the Nazis were extremely disciplined and would strictly manage all aspects of our daily lives, but the German invasion initially brought chaos to Sosnowiec. No one knew where to go or what to do. Should we work? Could we work? Is there school? Can we pray? Can we study? Should we go outside? Will they come banging on the door if we stay inside?

In the end, we went outside and stood in food lines for hours. Jews and Poles stood in the same lines at the beginning of the occupation. One day, I stood in line when an elderly Polish woman passing by called over a German soldier. She pointed at me and said "Jew." The soldier sent me to the back of the line and this elderly woman who I had never seen before took my place in line. The

---

5. The *Wehrmacht* was the United Armed Forces of Germany, consisting of the Army (Heer), Navy (Kriegsmarine), and Air Force (Luftwaffe).

German soldiers often could not tell the difference between Jews and Poles just by looking at us, but Poles could spot a Jew from a mile away. They often helped themselves by helping Nazis identify Jews; a kilo of sugar was awarded to any Pole who identified a Jew.

The disorder was brief. Regulations were put in place in quick succession. First, newspapers and radios were banned. Electric fans were next. I immediately burned all the newspapers we had in our home, as well as some of those same magazines with the photographs of burning synagogues that Max had pointed to when he furiously argued with his father about the capabilities of invading Germans. We kept our radio and fan. And then regretted that decision. Only a few days after the deadline for turning them in, my mother said we were crazy to put ourselves at risk for a little air circulation and to listen to German propaganda. I took a hammer to the fan and the radio and after smashing them into what I hoped were pieces small enough so that they were unrecognizable, I threw the pieces in the trash outside a Polish school on the other side of town.

The Nazis' next step was the establishment of the Judenrat in Sosnowiec, and installation of its offices at Targowa Street 12, a former home of the Rodamsker Rebbe. It was a large home, as unlike most Hasidic Rabbis, the Rodomsker Rebbe was a successful businessman in addition to being a Rabbi. His home in Sosnowiec was one of several homes he owned throughout Poland and Germany, and his yeshiva in Sosnowiec was one of many yeshivas that he supported with his personal funds.

Moshe Merin was appointed head of the Judenrat. Before the war, he did not play any leadership role in the Jewish community, but when the Nazis asked for a leader of the Jews to come forward, he volunteered. The Judenrat was basically a mini-government for the Jews under Nazi rule. It was responsible for supplies, food, healthcare, and property for the Jews of Sosnowiec, and for resettlement of Jewish refugees from other parts of Poland in Sosnowiec. It even had its own Jewish militia for enforcement. The militia headquarters was located directly across Targowa Street.

The Judenrat had over twenty members aside from Merin, but he alone controlled Jewish life under German occupation. He personally made decisions regarding employment assignments, forced labor selections, and most importantly, deportation lists. He was feared by the Jews of Sosnowiec and being on his good side could save one's life. He frequently accepted bribes and was not above putting his own wants over other peoples' needs.

CHAPTER 5

M Y FIRST WORK assignment from the Judenrat arrived in
late October of 1939. I was still working at my uncle's
roofing factory at the time, and as had become my
routine, I had stopped at the bakery on my way home from work to
see if there was any bread left at the end of the day. Sometimes I got
lucky and there was still a loaf or two available. That particular day,
I was disappointed to come home empty-handed but put a smile on
my face when I saw Herschel standing on the street in front of our
building.

"Aaron and I found this posted on the door when we arrived home
this afternoon," Herschel said as he handed me an envelope with my
name on it.

"Let's see what it is," I said, the smile still plastered onto my face.

It could not be good news. There was no good news to be delivered
these days. And even if there were, it would not be posted to the door
in an envelope with my name on the front. I must smile for as long
as I possibly can, I thought, for my brother's sake.

Inside the envelope was a formal notice of assignment to a labor
camp. I was to appear at a field near the outskirts of town the next
morning carrying only a single knapsack. Rumors had been circulating
about labor camps since shortly after the German invasion, but I was
among the first groups of Sosnowiec's Jews to be sent to such a camp.
The Judenrat told the Jewish community that if the young and healthy
went to work, children and the elderly would be permitted to stay
safely in Sosnowiec.

According to the notice, mine was a temporary work assignment that would last only a few weeks. My parents were devastated to see me go, but I went willingly, believing that I was saving the rest of my family. I did not have a choice anyway; it was too dangerous to disregard the notice and my parents did not have anything valuable enough for bribery, the only way out of a labor assignment.

So, the next morning, I said goodbye to my family and to Genia, packed clothing and food into my knapsack, and set off to the field. Approximately three hundred young men gathered in the field, some accompanied by entire families. I was glad my family stayed home. Too many parents were clinging tearfully to their sons. We climbed into German military trucks under the watchful eyes of Wehrmacht soldiers.

The trucks drove a familiar route toward Katowice, and I was thrilled when we slowed down as we entered the city. I was afraid we would be taken much further away. Genia had cousins who lived in Katowice, and I had an uncle and cousin who lived in Sosnowiec but were recently assigned by the Judenrat to a work brigade in Katowice sweeping the streets. Less than seven kilometers from home! We were lucky.

"Get out! Out!"

The soldiers yelled as we climbed out of the trucks, just outside the city.

"Line up! Rows of five! Five Jews per row! Five!"

We scrambled to set ourselves up into rows of five. I recognized two of the other young men in my row from school. We acknowledged each other silently and stood still in our row. A lot of the boys looked familiar to me. We were all between the ages of seventeen and twenty-two and came from the same city.

Just as we were organized into our rows of five, more Wehrmacht trucks approached. Four jeeps full of Gestapo[6] soldiers surrounded us: one jeep in front, one behind, and one on each side of our little formation. In what seemed like a choreographed effort, the Wehrmacht soldiers climbed into their trucks as the Gestapo soldiers exited their jeeps, and the Wehrmacht trucks drove off. We were left under the guard of the Gestapo.

---

6. The Gestapo (*Geheime Staatspolizei*), was the official secret police of Nazi Germany. Among its responsibilities was the roundup and deportation of Jews.

Then the real shouting began. I quickly learned that the Gestapo soldiers always yelled. They had no inside voices.

"March! March! Faster! Stay in Line! In Line!!"

We marched silently five deep through the streets of Katowice. Poles yelled and threw debris at us while we passed. Someone threw freezing water from a window above. If any Jews were watching, they did not acknowledge us. We marched through Katowice to a soccer field where we were joined by groups of young men around our age from Katowice and Chorzow. There, representatives of the Katowice Judenrat handed each of us a few coins and half a loaf of bread. I put the money in my pocket and added my bread to the food in my knapsack. By the time we organized ourselves into another, this time longer, five-column formation, the sun was setting. We turned around and marched back toward town, to the Katowice train station.

A boxcar train was waiting at the station. We boarded the train, each of us still carrying a small bag. We sat on the floor of the train as it sat still on the tracks. I was disappointed to learn that we would not be staying in Katowice after all. I fell asleep after a few hours of just waiting on the stationary train; I don't know how long we sat there before the train began to move or how long I slept on the moving train. I woke when the train stopped.

"We're in Nisko," one of the boys I did not recognize said as I stood up to stretch.

Nisko was a town near the Polish-Russian border. It is only about three hundred kilometers from Katowice to Nisko, but it was morning when we arrived. I had slept through the whole night on the train. The doors clanked open and again the Gestapo soldiers were yelling.

"Out! Out! Step down! Step down! Form a straight line with your backs to the train!"

We disembarked and lined up on the platform as directed. Across the platform there were passengers stepping out of what looked like a regular passenger train. They looked like a group of tourists from Western Europe heading to the mountains for a ski trip, wrapped in warm coats and wearing snow boots. They loaded their luggage onto buggies driven by Polish porters. They did not appear to notice the hundreds of young men standing at attention opposite them as we watched them organize themselves and their belongings.

The Gestapo soldiers began to yell at the travelers across the way.

That's when I realized they were not on vacation. The soldiers directed them out of the train station, and I watched them walk slowly, talking amongst themselves, no order or structure to be found. In a more characteristically Nazi display of movement, we young men were ordered to follow the unorganized mob of tourist-looking folks in yet another five-row formation.

We marched out of the train station and down a long road away from Nisko. It took just a few hours to reach the end of the road, where there was only mud ahead of us. The porters were told to turn around and the other group was forced to drive its own wagons. Some of us left our formation to help the Westerners with their belongings. As we trekked through mud, I learned from their accents that our fellow marchers were from Czechoslovakia. We approached a camp of some sort, a small collection of barracks that appeared partially built, but deserted. We marched straight through.

Shortly after we passed the camp, the soldiers suddenly stopped moving. The officer who seemed to be in charge of our peculiar mix of Polish boys and wealthy Czechoslovakians pointed ahead, said something in German I did not understand, and walked to the back of our group. We watched each of the other soldiers join him along his way to the rear until they were all standing behind us. We stood, a large group of disconnected Jews, in the middle of a muddy field, all with our backs to home and our eyes looking toward Russia.

"Go! Go! Go!" The soldiers yelled in unison from behind us.

That I understood. We continued to move forward while our guards remained at our rear. And then, chaos ensued. Our formation dissolved as people began running in all directions. I froze. I heard gunshots behind me and turned my head to look back. Those who tried to run back toward the direction from which we came were shot by the soldiers who were now behind us. A truck appeared, seemingly out of nowhere, and the Gestapo soldiers piled in and drove off.

"They left because their task is complete. They sent us out. The Nazis don't want us in Germany or in Poland." said a boy who was on my train from Katowice standing next to me.

It made sense. We were not going to work so that we could save our families. They were sending us to Russia. They wanted to get rid of the young men. They must have thought resistance was most likely from teenage boys and young men. We were most likely to fight. But the Nazis did not know me. They sent away the wrong guy. I was not a fighter.

CHAPTER 6

"I AM DR. BRENNER," BEGAN a tall, thin, well-dressed man in Czechoslovakian accented Yiddish, as he climbed onto the top of a wagon.

"As you can tell," he continued, "the Germans left. I suggest that we travel as a group to Russian occupied Poland."

There was something about Dr. Brenner that made me think we should listen to him. The Czechoslovakian contingent gathered around as he spoke. They seemed to look to him for direction, and he appeared to be a natural leader; he looked like someone who would keep us safe. I quickly decided to follow him.

Our crowd shrunk as groups broke off and went in different directions. Some more tried to head back toward the German occupied area, but that seemed like a bad idea to me given the gunshots I heard not that long ago. Some disappeared into the forest, and a few just sat around in the field, in the middle of the no man's land between the German and Russian forces in which we found ourselves. I stuck with Dr. Brenner and his group of about a hundred people. We passed in and out of small villages. The Czechs were as wealthy as I had thought. They were able to purchase food, and many were willing to share with those of us who were hungry. Some of them even had guns, which I never saw used, but they were certainly kept visible for protection.

After two or three days, we saw a sign for Russia. Almost as soon as I saw that sign, a German army jeep pulled up. We hadn't seen soldiers in days, but I saw the jeep directly in front of us and thought, just our luck. A patrol shows up as we were about to leave Germany. Dr. Brenner went over to the jeep and spoke to the soldiers inside. I have no idea what he said to them, but they drove off and left us alone. We continued to walk and in the early evening, arrived at what seemed to be the current border, a narrow river with a walking bridge above.

There were just two German soldiers on the German side of the bridge. Dr. Brenner had a short conversation with them, after which it was decided that we would stay on the German side until the morning. We spent the night on the German controlled side of the bridge, listening to the Russian soldiers sing folk songs while we waited until morning.

When the sun came up, more German soldiers approached Dr. Brenner and one spoke to him briefly.

"They will let us cross the border here," Dr. Brenner told the group, "but we must leave German territory forever. First, however, he will count us and take all our money and valuables. His fellow soldiers will then search us and whoever is found to have held back anything will not be permitted to leave, but instead be kept on this side of the border."

The soldiers surrounded us with guns raised as Dr. Brenner spoke, so I thought "be kept on this side of the border" probably meant something worse than just being sent back home. It did not matter for me personally. I had no valuables to give up. Even after the few days we spent wandering, the Czechs had plenty to hand over. I stood in line to be counted and continued on as we crossed the bridge in single file.

When we reached the other side, some of the Czechoslovakians kissed the ground. It confused me. I was happy to be out from under Nazi rule, but we were in Russia! The land of the pogrom! Not really kiss worthy if you ask me. I had mixed feelings. I was physically safe. But my family, and Genia, my whole life, were on the other side of the border, and I could not return. I sat down on the side of the road with my head in my hands.

"This is not a country of gold, and you are not in heaven."

I looked up as an old Russian officer spoke these words in Yiddish. I was sure he was right, but I had no choice but to get up and move. To somewhere. I could not sit on the side of the road forever. I may have been far away, but now that I was safe, I would do my best to figure out how to help my family.

The Russian soldiers took approximately thirty of the Czechs, including Dr. Brenner, into a building for questioning. The rest of us waited around drinking tea and eating crackers the Russians had provided. After a couple of hours, those questioned came out of the building surrounded by Russian soldiers. With no explanation, they rounded up the rest of us and walked us back toward German occupied Poland. We were back at the river, but instead of taking us over the bridge, the Russians led us to a shallow part of the river and watched us walk across the river in water almost waist deep.

Before I knew it, we were back on the German side. Dr. Brenner stood up on a big boulder and spoke again.

"The Russians are sending us back because they don't want any more refugees now," he said. "I do not know what will happen when the Germans find us back here. It is probably best if we all split up and do whatever we can to keep ourselves alive and safe. I wish you all the best of luck."

He stepped off the boulder and I never saw him again. Dr. Brenner's leadership got me through my first separation from family and the world that I had known before the war. I do not know whether Dr. Brenner survived or what became of him.

I was in shock. I was cold. My pants were frozen and stiff from the water. It began to rain, which only made us wetter and colder. I saw one of the boys I recognized from Sosnowiec, Dovid, sitting on the ground, crying. I joined him. I do not know how long we sat there and cried.

We stopped when a young boy who appeared to be about eleven or twelve approached us. He told us, in Yiddish, that he was Jewish, and we should come back with him to his home where we could warm up and get a hot meal before he helped us cross the border back into Russia. We learned that his father had been a shochet, a kosher butcher, who was killed by German soldiers when they found him helping other Jews trying to cross the border into Russia several weeks earlier. The boy lived with his mother, grandmother, and younger siblings just a short walk from the border. He, along with his mother and grandmother, had spent the last few weeks continuing his father's efforts to help Jews escape Nazi occupied Poland.

We followed him to his home, where we joined a roomful of

people eating hot soup in their underclothes. We too took off our cold, wet pants, and hung them to dry as we ate gratefully. We sat around, unable to sleep, for several hours. The boy, whose name I never learned, spoke with courage that defied his age, as he told us that we would cross the border in groups. He and some of his friends would lead us to different places along the border where they believed small groups could safely cross in the dark night.

I volunteered, along with Dovid, to be in the first group, thinking that we were better off leaving this no man's land between borders behind as soon as possible. The boy took six of us, all young men from our initial transport, including Dovid and me, back to the border as the rain that had begun the evening before intensified. He brought us to the site of a demolished bridge, where beams rising several feet above the water appeared to be all that remained. He disappeared for just a minute into some trees and returned with several long rectangular pieces of wood. The boy climbed up onto one of the beams and laid a piece of wood across until the next beam, creating a walkway over the water. He repeated the climb three more times, each time lengthening the walkway, until it reached all the way over the water, serving as a new bridge. The six of us then took turns crawling along the wooden boards, making it across the border just as the sun was coming up.

There was a small village just over the demolished bridge. We walked toward the village, staying close to the forest to avoid Russian soldiers. It was cold and dark. We passed a man carrying two buckets of milk who told us in Yiddish to keep walking and not stop until we were safely in the middle of the village.

Just as we arrived in what looked like the center of the village, a man called out to us from an open window, this time in Polish. He invited us into his home, where we learned that he too had escaped German-occupied Poland, but not because he was a Jew. He was a Polish communist afraid for his life under the Nazis, so he went to Russia just days after the invasion of Poland. At that point, it had been much easier to cross the border.

"Good morning. You're welcome to stay with me for as long as you would like," he said, "but the police are looking for refugees who crossed the border illegally and sending them back."

"We want to go to Lvov," Dovid responded. "I have family there and they may be able to help us."

It was the first I had heard of Dovid's family in Lvov, but it sounded like a good idea to me. My only other option was to stay with this communist stranger in his small village. I did not know Dovid well before we found each other at the Russian border, but at least when we were together, I felt less alone. We were connected to the same home.

The other young men with whom we had crossed the border with had no interest in going to Lvov. I do not know where they ended up, but I decided to go to Lvov with Dovid.

The Polish communist traveled with us to Lvov, just out of the goodness of his heart. He knew how to get there and how to speak Russian. We gave him nothing in return, and I never found out why he helped us. I was amazed by his generosity.

We did not even learn his name, just as we did not learn the name of the young boy who helped us cross the border into Russia. It felt odd, being the recipient of tremendous help from strangers. I made a promise to myself on the way to Lvov - no matter what I encountered in Lvov or throughout my life, I would help others in need.

CHAPTER 7

L VOV HAD BEEN a Polish city until September of 1939, when the Red Army invaded and claimed it as part of the Soviet Union. We arrived during a very well attended parade. There were red flags everywhere and posters of Stalin on street corners. The parade was meant to commemorate a Soviet historical event that held no significance for most of the inhabitants of Lvov, which had only recently become part of the Soviet Union. Thousands of people were on the streets, but few of the spectators appeared enthusiastic. We later learned that most of them were there because the Russians required workers to attend celebratory Soviet events.

Dovid and I watched the parade while we tried to figure out how we could find his relatives. He had two cousins in Lvov, his father's brother's sons, who both left Sosnowiec just after the Germans invaded and were able to get across the Russian border when it was easily passed. Dovid was sure they would help us, if only we could find them.

"My cousins are both religious," Dovid said, "we should start by finding shuls and see if anyone there knows them."

Dovid stopped a man who looked like us, clearly a refugee, and asked in Yiddish, where we may find a synagogue.

"A synagogue?" he asked, "there is one on almost every corner of the Jewish section of Lvov. There must be almost fifty, if you count the really small ones. Why do you want a synagogue? Morning prayers were over hours ago."

"We are looking for my cousins. They came here at the beginning of September, and we are hoping they can help us find work and someplace to stay," Dovid answered.

"I am Selig," the man said, as he extended his hand to shake Dovid's and then mine. "It is difficult to find anyone in this city. Refugees in Lvov number in the tens of thousands, and more arrive every single day. I just got here a week ago. Lucky to get over the border. There was a single Russian soldier on guard when I arrived at the border. He must have had too much to drink and was passed out when I crossed. The best place to start looking for your cousins, and for the two of you to get yourselves settled, is the refugee office."

We followed Selig's directions to the refugee office. The man standing behind the counter at the office handed us each a pencil and a form to fill out. It was a basic form that asked for only three things: Name, Birthdate, and City of Origin. We returned our completed forms and without a word, the man handed us a card with an address on it.

"Can you help me find someone?" Dovid asked. "My cousins are here in Lvov, and I would like to find them."

"There are thousands of refugees in Lvov," the man behind the counter replied. "You can post a note on that board, and maybe they will come looking for you."

He gestured toward a wall covered in handwritten notes as he handed Dovid back the pencil, a small piece of paper, and a pin to attach his note to the wall. Then he turned his back and went through a door behind his counter.

Dovid wrote something on the paper, stuck it on the wall, and stood there, staring at the paper for several minutes before he came back over to where I was standing.

"I don't think I will ever find them. They don't even know I am here. Why would they come looking?"

"Maybe someone else they know will come looking for another refugee, and they will tell your cousins you're here and looking for them. Did you write the address of the refugee house where we are going so that they can find you if they learn that you're here?"

"Yes."

"Then let's go over there. Maybe we can come up with some other ways to find them when we get to wherever refugees are housed. You can't be the only one looking for relatives. There must be a way to find them other than that single wall inside this office."

I wasn't sure if there really was another way to find Dovid's cousins, but I wanted to give him (and me) some hope that we would be able to find them and that they would be able to help us.

We walked out onto the street and asked another seeming refugee to direct us toward the address we had been given. We followed his instructions and a few blocks later found ourselves standing in front of a big building with thick wooden doors. As soon as we stepped inside, a Russian-speaking woman approached, showed us to a corner in a large room, and pointed to the bare floor.

"This is where you'll be sleeping. There is water out the back door," she said quickly and walked away before we had a chance to ask about Dovid's cousins or even whether there was somewhere we might get a blanket.

We walked through the house to get outside, passing through an awkward combination of large rooms and narrow hallways. There were about fifty men spread out around the house, some sitting around talking, some sleeping, and a few just standing on their own staring off into space. Watching those men on their own made me sad. They looked so lost and alone. I was happy to have Dovid with me then. At least I wasn't completely alone.

Once outside, we saw what the woman had meant by "water out the back door." There was a single outhouse with a toilet and a single pump for water.

"One toilet for all of these men?" I asked no one in particular.

"One toilet for double the number of men you saw as you walked through the house. Half of the men are at work." The woman from inside had appeared beside me and answered.

"We do what we can," she continued, "but the number of refugees keeps growing and growing, and there is nowhere to accommodate them. Almost every family in Lvov has relatives from other places or even strangers living with them at this point."

She went on to explain how the Christians of Lvov were housing refugees along with their Jewish neighbors, and that there was simply no more space in the city. The Russians were sending people by train further into the Soviet Union with promises of better living conditions, jobs, and prepaid wages, just to manage the population. It sounded somewhat appealing to get on a train and put even more distance between myself and the Nazis, but I knew I could not bear to go further away from home.

As refugees who were provided with housing by the Soviet government, Dovid and I were expected to work. I was assigned to clean the bombed-out railroad station. Each morning, I woke up before dawn so that I could use the toilet and wash myself with fresh water from the pump before the lines were too long. Then, I walked a short distance from where we were staying to the train station, where a Russian soldier handed me a broom. I spent hours with a small group of refugees cleaning debris out of the railroad station. I learned that the main train station in Lvov had been a modern, three-story building with all of the newest technology before it was partially destroyed by German bombs on September 1, 1939.

The Russians treated us well. We were given several breaks a day as well as food for breakfast and lunch. But the work was difficult, and I was surprised to find, after a full week of work, that we were not paid at all. I was happy to eat breakfast and lunch while at work, but how was I going to eat dinner or find some way out of refugee housing if I did not make any money? There was certainly no way I could help anyone at home without money.

I walked back to the refugee house determined to find another way. I would talk to Dovid and come up with another plan. I worked mornings and Dovid worked afternoons so we only saw each other in passing that week. Dovid was assigned to a job in the refugee office where we had first registered. He was thrilled with that assignment, hopeful that it would help him find his cousins. I wondered how his week had been and looked forward to catching up as we both had the next day off from work.

I walked back to the house as I had every day that week, stood on the water pump line, and washed myself as well as I could under the circumstances. Then I went inside and played cards with two other Polish refugees while we discussed how none of the refugees here in Lvov get paid for their work. I put down my cards and approached Dovid as soon as he walked in the door.

"We need to find another way, Dovid. I can't imagine continuing to work for free. I've asked around and found out that none of the refugees get paid. There are men who have been living in this house for a couple of months with no money at all, and no way out. I came to Russia for this?"

"But we must," Dovid answered. "We don't have a choice. Unless you want to get on one of those trains that takes us even further away from anyone we know. We must stay. We are lucky to have our small corner to sleep in this house. There are so many others sleeping wherever they can, even on park benches. We will find my cousins and they will help us."

"I can't," I told him.

I knew Dovid was partially right – there were people sleeping on park benches. And at least with Dovid I did not feel all alone. But I also knew that it was time to move on. He had family in Lvov, so I understood why he wanted to stay. If I thought it would bring me closer to my family, I too would have stayed and lived in a house with a hundred other men and just a single toilet. I would even have slept on a park bench. But I needed to do something. At the very least, I needed to make a life for myself while I figured out how to help my family.

That evening, I went to a coffee house that served as an informal meeting place for Jewish refugees. I had to find someone there who could point me in another direction – a paying job, a better place to live, news from home. Something.

I sat down at an empty table by the kitchen and people-watched for a while. It was a motley crew. Men, women, old, young, bearded men, men without head coverings, all together in this coffee house. My grandfather would have loved to see this place. He had always told me that all Jews should accept one another and focus on our similarities, not our differences. Here we were, different in so many ways, but together in misery.

Thinking of my grandfather motivated me. I got up from my seat and walked over to a table across the room where three men dressed in black were already sitting. My parents were observant Jews, but not as strict as my grandparents. My grandfather looked like the Hasidic Jew he was, and these men looked like younger versions of my grandfather – long beards, heads covered, long black coats.

"Good evening," I said in Yiddish, as I sat down in an empty chair at their table. "My name is Kalman Sztajer."

They each introduced themselves. They too were refugees from Poland. They had come to Lvov just before the war. They planned to take a train further into Russia the next day to study at a small yeshiva there. They couldn't help me. My high hopes of figuring out a grand plan to do something, anything, were quickly dashed. We chatted for a few minutes, and I left, disappointed.

I was not supposed to stay at the refugee house if I did not work, but they were not particularly organized. It would take at least a few days for anyone to figure out that I was still sleeping there but had stopped going to work. I spent the next three days walking around Lvov and the evenings talking to other refugees in the coffee house. I ate lunch at a soup kitchen all three days. It was my only meal of the day and a harsh reminder of my past life. I had fallen from a dispenser of sandwiches to my own needy classmates to a recipient of free food in such a short time.

On my fourth evening at the coffee house, I finally found what I had been looking for. In walked my old neighbor!

"Sam!" I yelled his name as I ran to greet him. Sam was a couple of years older than me and grew up in the same building as my cousins, just down the block from mine. He had left Sosnowiec just a few days before we met in Lvov. Sam was a great guy, kind, and fun to be around. He was also an only child whose parents spoiled him; he was used to getting his way. His parents were frightened for Sam's future and paid a smuggler to bring him to Lvov. I was thrilled to see him, but my happiness was fleeting as he caught me up on recent events at home.

He began by pulling an armband out of his coat pocket.

"We have to wear this now at home. All of the Jews of Sosnowiec and nearby places like Bezdin and Katowice wear white and blue armbands. We must carry identification cards at all times. And they are taking Jews away from Sosnowiec."

"Taking them away? Where?"

"Nobody knows. As of when I left town just a few days ago, your family was all at home. There are other people, people you know, good people, even children, Kalman, who have been just thrown into the backs of German trucks, driven away, and not heard from since."

"Have you heard anything about the Ecksteins?"

"Genia was home as of when I left. Only Mr. Eckstein was taken, but he is one of the few who returned."

I took a deep breath as he continued.

"Last month, the Gestapo arrested approximately one hundred Jewish men from Sosnowiec and Bedzin. They chose only the wealthiest and most important and held them until their families came together and paid an outrageous ransom. They were all returned to their homes. Since then, random Jews have been taken out of their homes and workplaces and off the streets, and none of them have been seen since."

I knew life could not be good at home, but I hadn't expected this. It was the push I needed. I told Sam I was going home. He tried to convince me to stay. He had brought enough money to stay in Lvov for a while and had even found himself a private room to rent. He offered to share the room and his money with me so that I too could get settled. But seeing Sam reminded me that I could not remain in Lvov. Sam's parents wanted him out of Poland, but I knew my place was with my family. I was going home.

"I must go," I told Sam.

Less than an hour after greeting Sam, I hugged him again and said goodbye. I agreed to borrow some money from him for my journey and promised Sam I would visit his parents when I got home and let them know that he was safe in Lvov.

I walked back to the refugee house with a new sense of purpose. By going home, I was quite literally heading into dangerous territory, but I felt both at peace and excited. I picked up all the clothing I had – somehow, I had accumulated a few additional articles of clothing while in Lvov – and brought them with me to a public bathhouse. There, I showered and had all my clothing disinfected. Then, I put every single piece of clothing on my body and walked over to the railroad station I had swept just a few days earlier.

CHAPTER 8

THE TRAIN STATION was crowded with people heading deeper into Russia. I bought a ticket for the opposite direction, for a town near the Russian/German border, which was changing daily. My ride was much longer than it would have been if not for detours required by the Russian army, but otherwise uneventful. When I got off the train the next morning, however, I was hit with the realization that I left Lvov without a real plan. I couldn't very well just walk over to the German border guards and tell them I had been deported to Russia but decided to return home.

A heavyset man approached me almost as soon as I exited the train and offered to smuggle me over the German border for a fee. He gestured to three other young men and told me he would get us all across that night. I did not have any other options and I figured that if this fellow picked me out as confused and somewhat helpless within minutes of stepping off the train, I would not last long on my own before German soldiers caught me.

I paid him more than half of the money Sam had given me and hid in a storage room behind a small wood workshop along with the three other men. One was a Polish man, a former soldier from Krakow, who was heading home to see his dying father. The other two were Jews from Bendin who were also returning home to be with their families. We sat inside the small room all day, until finally, a few hours after sundown, the heavyset man returned. He pointed us in what he said was the direction of an unguarded section of the border and off we went. We walked for hours under a full moon. By the time the sun

48

rose, we realized we had been swindled. He had sent us further into Russian territory.

Shortly after sunrise, we were caught by Russian soldiers. Lucky for us, the former Polish soldier spoke Russian and explained to our captors that we had just escaped Germany. They believed his explanation that we had snuck across the border into Russian territory the previous night and spent the night walking east. They would force us back over the border to the German side.

They ordered us into their jeep and drove us directly to the border, where they told us to cross into German territory. I am not sure where the German border guards were, but we walked across as though there was no border at all. A few miles past what seemed to be the border we ran into a small group of German soldiers who did not ask us any questions. They waved us over when they saw us, which made my stomach drop. Then, they asked us to help them pull their sled over a small hill, said thank you, and waved us off. I have no idea who they thought we were, what they thought we were doing there, or if they were even thinking at all.

We quickly made our way to the nearest train station and found a train scheduled to stop in Cmielow. Cmielow was a small town over two hundred kilometers from Sosnowiec, but we chose that train because it was the first one heading into the German-occupied side of Poland. We would figure out how to get home when we were on the right side of the border.

It was dark when we got off the train and went to a small shop where I used Sam's money to treat my companions to coffee and sweet rolls. We sat on a bench to eat, and a middle-aged man sat down next to me. I was wary of strangers after being swindled at the last train station, so I inched away slightly as he sat down.

"Where are you gentlemen heading?" he asked.

"Bendin," replied one of my companions as I remained quiet.

"You people should not go there. They will catch you and kill you," he answered matter-of-factly. "You should stay here. Do you know anyone in Cmielow?"

"My second cousin is married to the eldest daughter of the Bloom family," I said.

I still was not sure about this man, so I gave him some vague but true information that I thought wouldn't hurt to share.

"Izak?" he asked. "Izak is your cousin? Izak is a good friend of mine. Take this and travel with it. And make sure you go through Krakow. Don't go directly from here to Bendin."

"Krakow works," said one of the guys from Bendin, as he pointed to the Polish soldier with whom we traveled.

"This guy is from Krakow," he continued, "and my aunt lives there. Maybe she can help us get back home."

I looked down at his hand and saw that Izak's friend was handing me his identification papers. His papers! I refused to take them, thinking of the trouble he could get into for not having them with him. But we listened to his advice and exchanged our tickets for new ones, for passage directly to Krakow, even though the trip would be several hours longer.

The train ride to Krakow was uneventful, but our arrival was jarring. We walked out of the train station to the sound of German soldiers yelling.

"Jews! Jews! Jews!" Just that single word repeated over and over as the German soldiers grabbed whoever wore a white and blue armband and shoved them into trucks. Men, women, and children were all screaming in the chaos. They were taking everyone. But no luggage. Possessions were just left on the ground as the trucks filled up and departed one by one. I had no idea where those trucks were going but I knew I did not want to be on one.

I bent and picked up an armband I saw on the ground. It must have fallen off a fellow Jew in the chaos. I stuck it in my coat pocket just in case I needed it at some point. In the commotion, I made my way unnoticed to a horse carriage, along with the two men on their way to Bendin. I have no idea what came over me, but I stuck my finger in my pocket as though I had a gun inside. I informed the Polish driver that we were members of the Polish underground and needed to go to the address of my companion's aunt. I told him that other members of the underground were watching us in case he was thinking of going to the authorities.

I was shocked. I could not believe what I had done. I was Kalman, the steady rule follower, the guy who puts his head down and does what he is told. Most importantly, I was honest and kind. I just nearly scared a man to death pretending that I had a gun and that I would use it! My traveling companions had no reason to be surprised. They did not know me before I became the guy who terrified an innocent stranger by pretending to have a gun. I have no idea where the courage came from in that moment. Maybe it was necessity or maybe just plain fear of the alternative. Either way, we arrived safely at the address I had given the driver, and my companions jumped out of the carriage immediately. I lingered for a moment and considered apologizing. I wanted so badly to confess, but I did not. I would have given us away.

We spent the night at the aunt's house in Krakow. It turned out she had no way to help us obtain identification papers, so we headed back to the train station in the morning with no papers and no real plan other than to get on a train to Sosnowiec and hope no one checked for papers along the way. We bought tickets for the train to Sosnowiec and boarded early, hoping not to be caught up in the mass of Jews at the train station. The three of us sat down together, and before the conductor had a chance to ask for tickets, a German soldier began walking through the train.

"Any Jews here?" he asked repeatedly.

We did not answer, and remained seated. We were likely the only Jews on the train, and it felt like the other passengers, all appearing to be Polish, were staring at us. They knew we were Jews and must have thought we were crazy for being on that train. Without a word to each other, we stood up, got off the train and walked in different directions on the platform. I turned to my left and walked toward the front of the train without looking back to see where the others went.

In the back window of the train's second car, I saw a German soldier sitting by himself, sleeping. I walked into that car with my armband still safely in my pocket and sat a few rows in front of him. I closed my eyes, pretending to be asleep as well. The lights went on as the conductor came into the car asking for tickets. He entered from the back of the car and spent a minute or two waking the soldier to collect his ticket. Then, he walked through the car toward me. I was terrified. He poked me in the arm until I opened my eyes, and as I stuck my hand in my pocket as though reaching for a ticket, a voice from the back of the car yelled in German.

"It's time to go. Start the train."

The soldier had spoken. The conductor immediately walked away, and I closed my eyes again. This time in relief. I was accidentally saved by a German soldier. I had almost been caught and ended up on one of those trucks.

CHAPTER 9

W HEN THE TRAIN stopped in Sosnowiec, I ran home as quickly as I could. It was less than a mile and I made it home in minutes. I rang the building bell, and our Polish super opened the door.

"I'm home. I'm home!" I yelled as I raced past him up the stairs. My mother opened the door just as I reached the landing and hugged me. It was a happy homecoming. Looking back, my parents should not have been so happy that I was back in Poland. If they had any idea what was coming, they would have been furious at me for returning, not thrilled to see me.

In the morning, Herschel went over to the Ecksteins' apartment to tell Genia I was home. I had to remain in hiding until I figured out what to do. I had been deported so now found myself in German territory illegally, without identification papers. If I just walked into the Judenrat office to register, someone would notice that I was home. I did not leave our apartment for a week. It felt good to be home, but hard to idly sit around, helpless, and watch my family struggle. In the few months that I was gone, the lives of Jews in Sosnowiec had changed for the worse, and quickly.

There were almost too many restrictions to count. Jews had to follow a strict curfew. Jewish bank accounts were closed. Jewish businesses were required to be managed by Germans. Jews could not own fur coats. Jews could not own jewelry. Jews could not read newspapers. Jews had to step off sidewalks into the gutters to allow for non-Jews to pass. There were some streets that Jews were not permitted to walk on at all. That was particularly complicated for those Jews who lived on such streets, forcing some to literally cut holes in the walls of their homes so that they could enter or exit on a side street where their presence was permissible. Jews were forced to wear armbands. The list went on. And on.

About a week after my return, my uncle reached out to a former schoolteacher, a Jewish man who somehow was able to "get things done," as they say. People who could "get things done" had become quietly known around town. There were people who had access to the black market for food, illegal papers, and even American dollars. The teacher took me to the Judenrat office where the clerk behind the desk pretended to have no idea who I was even though she lived in Genia's building and I had known her for as long as I could remember. She prepared identification papers for me that showed I was registered as a resident of my aunt's home, just down the block from my own. She did not change my name. Then we went straight to the German police precinct where they took my fingerprints. I had identification papers to show I was once again a legal resident of Sosnowiec.

That meant I had papers to show German soldiers who stopped me in the street, a ration card for food, and employment potential. The Judenrat offered me a job as a policeman. One of the officers knocked on our door the day after I received my new set of papers. When I opened it, he reached out with a smile, a blue and white hat and specialty armband in his hand.

"What's this?" I asked him, looking down at his hand. I knew very well what it was.

"Your armband and hat. We don't have full uniforms, but they will identify you as a member of the Jewish police. You will receive a salary and increased rations, and of course, protection for your family."

I returned his smile, leaving the hat and armband in his outstretched hand.

"Thank you, but I am not interested. I'll find another job with fewer benefits."

He left and I closed the door slowly behind him. There was no way I could perform that job. I wanted to survive and to help my family, but not by causing someone else pain. I would not police my fellow Jews for the Nazis. No way.

But I did have to find another job, or I would find myself on the back of a truck soon. I went back to the Judenrat office the next day and simply told the clerk that I needed a job. I did not mention the policeman's visit, and without incident was assigned a job building cabinetry at a furniture factory once belonging to a Jewish family, but now owned by a local Pole. It was the same factory my father worked at.

At that point, the Judenrat operated a Jewish market and Jewish bakery. The Germans provided food and supplies that the Judenrat distributed to Jews based on their ration cards. There was never enough. Those who were lucky were able to sell whatever they had on the black market to buy food, but for those who had nothing to sell, the Judenrat ran a soup kitchen. For a while, Jews were also able to grow produce on a plot of land provided by the Nazis and divided into family plots by the Judenrat. One day, some Gestapo soldiers rounded up all the Jews working their land and sent them on one of those trucks. From then on, Jews were afraid to farm there, and the land was left untouched.

All Jews were forced to work for meager pay. I was able to buy six small rolls of bread on the black market with a full week's pay at the furniture factory. Those six rolls literally cost all the money I made each week.

My brothers worked at a small leather goods factory, as children as young as eight were forced to work. Those who did not work were likely to be thrown in the back of a truck never to be seen from again. And although it helped, even a job did not offer complete protection. At that point, one's ability to stay in Sosnowiec depended on any one man at any given time. Any German soldier could decide, at any point, that you were to be sent away or even shot. Plenty of Jews with jobs were thrown into trucks.

CHAPTER 10

W E CONTINUED TO work and live that way for several months. Food became increasingly scarce, the sick got sicker, and more Jews disappeared. Families were torn apart, but my family was still together and relatively healthy. My parents, sister, brothers, and I were all working and making do as best we could under the circumstances.

In the fall of 1940, I got another notice of deportation from the Judenrat. This time, the notice said exactly where I was going – to Annaburg. I had three days to pack, say my goodbyes, and be at the train station. I was, according to my notice, being given the honor of building the Reich's Autobahn.[7]

I set off, knowing that ignoring the notice would put my entire family in danger. The scene at the train station was similar to the one I encountered when I first left Sosnowiec the year before. I, on the other hand, was wiser. It was warm outside, but I wore three layers of clothing and heavy work boots as I walked to the train station. When the train arrived, dripping in sweat, I boarded with a group of young Jewish men, some of whom had lived in Sosnowiec their entire lives, and some of whom were from neighboring towns but had been sent to Sosnowiec when they were evicted from their own

---

7. Beginning in 1940, the Schmelt Organization, led by Brigadeführer Albrecht Schmelt, controlled forced labor camps where Jews worked on construction of the Autobahn. Annaburg was one of over 177 labor camps in the Schmelt Organization, which originally supported highway construction, and were later used for armaments and industrial needs.

homes. It seemed that the new Jews were arriving in Sosnowiec from other parts of Poland daily.

The train was a typical passenger one. We boarded the train in an orderly fashion, presenting our deportation notices to the SS[8] guard at the train's entrance, as though he were a conductor collecting tickets. After an unmemorable trip, we disembarked at Annaburg, were each given a uniform and a bar of soap, and assigned to our barracks.

For the second time, the Nazis lumped me together with other men around my age. The first time it was to get rid of us by sending us to Russia, but this time, it was to use us to their advantage, building the Autobahn. The youngest and strongest among us, like me, were given the most taxing work, breaking up and moving heavy stone. And some of us took on even more work. Each man was assigned a section to work daily, and when those of us who were able finished early, we switched places with weaker men and completed their sections too. As long as the work was complete, no one cared one way or another about how the Jews got it done.

The labor was hard, but life at Annaburg was tolerable. We were supervised by German civilians, and worked alongside Polish civilians who, unlike us, were paid for their labor. We reported to the civilian foremen, while the Nazi guards seemed to be there just to make sure we did not escape. We marched to the worksite each morning singing Hebrew songs, were permitted periodic showers, and given a full slice of bread and cup of soup each day. The food was certainly lacking, but we were fed enough to work. We were permitted to walk around the camp freely when we were not at work and had the day off on Sundays. We were able to communicate with our families. The Judenrat provided us with stamps to send censored letters home, and we were able to receive packages. My parents sent just one package while I was there; it contained two pairs of long underwear and a box of cigarettes. My parents and Genia sent postcards frequently, and I was comforted knowing they were safe. Annaburg had an infirmary staffed by a Jewish doctor, Jewish dentist, and Jewish nurse.

---

8. The SS (Schutzstaffel, meaning "Protective Echelon," abbreviated) which began as Hitler's personal bodyguard unit, eventually assumed responsibility for, among other things, neutralizing opposition to Nazi Germany, enforcing its racial policies, and running labor camps and death camps.

Medication and supplies were scarce, but they did the best they could to care for sick or injured men under the circumstances.

One afternoon, after I'd been at Annaburg for almost a year, a German foreman called my name as we marched through the camp gates at the end of a workday.

"You're going home," he said, as I approached him.

"Go get your things and come back to the gate. The bus stops here in ten minutes. You'll get on and take it home."

And just like that, after almost a year, I was going home. I ran to my barrack, packed my small bag, and hurried back to the gate. I did not even say goodbye to the men I had lived with and worked with at Annaburg. I could not wait to get on that bus.

A bus stopped precisely when the guard said it would and I climbed on quickly. The Nazis were always punctual. It was mostly empty, with a few tired looking Jews who were spread out among the seats. I assumed they were picked up from the camps surrounding Annaburg, but I did not get a chance to speak to them. I fell asleep as soon as I sat down and slept the entire ride, through the night.

CHAPTER 11

"OUT! OUT, JEWS!"

I woke up to yelling. It did not even phase me anymore. It certainly could not put a damper on my excitement to be back home. I slowly exited the bus and found myself in the middle of Sosnowiec before sunrise. I was not far from Genia's apartment, but I did not want to go over there and wake anyone, so I walked home instead.

My father was already awake. He opened the door as I climbed the stairs and embraced me tightly, silently, for what felt like a very long time. When he let go, I looked at him through tears and asked, "Why are you awake?"

"I knew you would be here. I asked them to send you home."

I laughed. He asked them to send me home? Really? Sure. A Jewish dad asked the Nazis to send his son home and here I was!

"The truth please, Father. Why am I home?"

"The truth is that I asked them to send you home. About six months ago I was assigned a new job. I am doing construction work, overseeing a crew of Jews renovating apartments and offices for the Gestapo in Sosnowiec. There are several offices that must be renovated for a new group of SS officers who will be based in Sosnowiec. Yesterday, when the supervising officer reprimanded me for not working quickly enough, I told him that we would be able to move much more quickly if we had an experienced carpenter, and that I knew such a carpenter, my son. I said you were in Annaburg, and swore to him that with your help, I would have the offices ready on time. His response, barked at me as he walked away, was to expect you this morning and that you'd better get right to work."

It was not a joke after all. I did have some building and carpentry experience, working for my uncle's roofing company and at the furniture factory before I was sent to Annaburg. We ate breakfast, which consisted of a slice of bread and a very weak cup of tea, I changed my clothing, and we were off to work before the rest of my family awoke.

On the way to work, my father gave me a brief update of the goings on I had missed at home. It was more of the same, only worse. The Nazis were meaner and more brutal, and the Jews were poorer, sicker, and fewer than they had been when I left. Thankfully, my parents and brothers were still relatively healthy, as were Genia and her parents.

Julia and Genia's brothers were another story. They had not been taken by the Nazis. They ran away. To Russia. No one had heard from them in several months.

My father told me the story on the way to work, and Genia filled in the gaps when I went to see her that afternoon. It started with Henry. Henry had a best friend who was engaged to a beautiful girl. One low-ranking Nazi officer took a liking to this girl and began to follow her around, flirt with her, and even bring her small gifts. She was not interested, but he was not willing to take no for an answer. One evening, shortly before curfew, Henry was on his way to meet his best friend when he stumbled upon a scene straight out of a film.

Henry was supposed to meet this couple on the west side of Promenade Street. Henry heard his friend yell a panicked "No!" as he approached their meeting spot and quickly crouched down behind a truck, able to see the street but hidden from view. Henry turned his head to the right and saw his friend. His friend's left hand was up in the air saying "stop" while his right arm was wrapped behind him holding on to his girlfriend as she pressed up against his back. Henry turned his head to the left and saw that same low-ranking Nazi officer approach from the opposite end of the street, his gun pointed directly at Henry's friend. And then, without any provocation, the Nazi shot Henry's best friend in the chest.

The Nazi proceeded to attack his friend's fiance as she screamed in terror. He hit her with the gun that was still in his hand and began to rip at her clothing. At first, Henry just watched as he hid, frozen in shock and fear. And then, as anyone who knew Henry would have expected, he acted. He charged at the Nazi and pulled him away. They fought, trading punches, and rolling around on the ground, and as they struggled, Henry took hold of the gun. He stood up, pointed the gun at the Nazi who was trying to crawl away, and fired. Then he dropped the gun and ran straight home.

That is the story Henry told his father when he arrived at home.

"I shot a Nazi," he said as soon as he walked through the door, his voice and body trembling. His father looked up from the book he was reading.

"You what?"

"You heard me, Father. I shot a Nazi."

"Shot him dead?"

"I do not know. I did not stay long enough to find out."

Henry told his father the full story, and Mr. Eckstein knew that there was no way for this situation to end well. Henry could not stay. He had to leave. What if the Nazi was still alive and could identify him? What if someone else had seen him? What if he actually killed a Nazi?

"You must leave. Now. And take your brothers with you. If he is alive or if someone did see you shoot him and you disappear, they will come looking for Sol or Max in your place. Let's hope no one can identify you. Fingers crossed. You must all leave as soon as curfew ends tomorrow morning. It's too risky to leave at night. Just being three Jewish men on the street after curfew is cause for them to take you away."

They woke Sol and Max and told them the plan. The brothers would head for the Russian border and hope for the best. There was no time to find another option.

Soon after Germany had invaded, the Ecksteins had hidden some jewelry under a tile behind the stove. That night, Mr. Eckstein removed the tile, took almost all of the valuables he had stashed away and put it in a backpack they would bring with them on the journey. They shared the single backpack, knowing that three Jewish men traveling through German-occupied Poland with travel bags would surely appear suspicious.

Shortly before dawn, Mr. Eckstein woke his wife and broke the news to her; she had to say goodbye to all three of her sons. There was no other choice. The Ecksteins were devastated, as was Genia when she woke up to the commotion and found out her brothers were leaving. It was a heart-wrenching goodbye. At the time, Genia thought they were leaving because they had advance notice of their impending deportation to a labor camp. No one told Genia that Henry had shot a Nazi. It would be better if she did not know, just in case someone came around asking questions. By the time I got home from Annaburg, she knew all the details.

On their way out of the city, Max stopped to say goodbye to Julia. That turned out not to be a goodbye because Julia insisted on joining them. She dressed in two layers of clothing, three pairs of socks, and her warmest boots. My father, standing in his pajamas, held Julia's head in his hands and cried as he spoke.

"May God make you like Sarah, Rebecca, Rachel, and Leah. May God bless you and protect you. May God shine His face on you and be gracious to you. May God turn His face to you and grant you peace."[9]

Julia hugged my parents and brothers as she too cried and then followed Max out the door. The whole scene lasted only a few minutes.

They left and my father opened the door after it had closed behind them. As the four of them walked down the building stairs my father called out.

"Max! Julia!"

"Yes," they said in unison as they looked up. Julia's face was wet with tears.

"As soon as you get to Russia find a Rabbi and get married. Please, promise me you will be married by a Rabbi," he said.

And then he shut the door. Months later, as I pieced together the story from what my father and Genia told me, no one had heard from them. We had no idea where they were or if they were even alive.

---

9. It is a custom for Jewish parents to bless their children on Shabbat evening with a priestly blessing. Here, Nachum recited the priestly blessing for daughters.

CHAPTER 12

A FTER OUR ELDER siblings left, life continued to deteriorate for the Jews of Sosnowiec and for our families in particular. Our parents were distraught and seemed to be aging rapidly before our eyes, especially the Ecksteins. My parents were struggling with life under the Nazis generally, and with anxiety about Julia's wellbeing, in particular. But they still had two children to care for and continued to work every day. The Ecksteins were literally worried sick. No longer able to work, they stayed at home just hoping for news about their sons, and that no one would come for them and take them away. Mr. Eckstein had been a community leader, an astute businessman, and a demanding boss, and was now reduced to a shell of his former self. He sat at home all day, sometimes crying for his sons for hours on end.

It was up to Genia and me to support our parents. Roles were reversed. We were in charge. We ran our families' households as our parents slowly fell apart under Nazi rule. We were scared for them. We were afraid they would be taken away and not survive whatever awaited them, but we were also afraid that they would break right there at home. Despair and illness surrounded us in Sosnowiec, and we simply did not think they could take much more. Through rumors, stolen newspapers, and whispers throughout town, we slowly learned more about what the future held for Europe's Jews; from ghettos, to labor camps, to death camps, the future was increasingly ominous.

Life quickly went further downhill in the spring and summer of 1942, when the first large-scale deportations of Sosnowiec's Jews began. At the end of April 1942, a few thousand Jews received notice that they were to appear at Sosnowiec's soccer arena on May 10 for "resettlement." All the Jewish organizations in Sosnowiec called upon the Jews to resist by not reporting to the arena. They succeeded. Only a small group of Jews showed up, and the Gestapo forced Merin, the head of the Judenrat, and his militia to round up the rest of the Jews to meet the Nazi's quota. Two days later, 1,500 Jews from Sosnowiec were taken by train to Auschwitz.

In June, another group was summoned for deportation, this time to an old school building. Once again, many of those summoned failed to appear, and the Judenrat met that month's quota by rounding up residents of a nursing home, an orphanage, and a hospital. I heard that the sick and elderly who were unable to walk to the school were dragged there in wagons. This group headed straight to Auschwitz as well, and it became increasingly likely that those of us left behind would eventually meet the same fate. When the weak and the helpless were gone, deportation quotas would have to be met somehow, and even strong young men like me – who were useful to the Nazis for now because of our work – would end up on those cattle trains.

We lived on eggshells that summer. Each morning I left to work knowing that my family and Genia may not be there when I got home. The stress was eating at me, but I had no choice. I had to be strong for them.

There were no large-scale deportations in July. The Nazis must have been gearing up for August. All of the Jews still in Sosnowiec were ordered to assemble at the soccer arena on the morning of August 12, supposedly so that we could each re-register and obtain a special stamp on our identification cards. Those of us with jobs went to work that morning and marched to the arena, under guard, around midday. There were already thousands of Jews there when we arrived. The heat and humidity were oppressive. There was no food or water. Several people fainted, and by mid-afternoon, the Judenrat brought bread into the arena for distribution. Chaos quickly unfolded as a mass of starving, exhausted people descended upon the bread.

The Gestapo intervened and their rubber batons dissipated the mob. The entire arena was surrounded on all sides by SS men and the selection began. We stood in line, by family, and waited as a group of men led by SS Obersturmbahnführer Heinrich Lindner sent those assembled to the four corners of the arena. It was a relief that the Nazis seemed to be keeping families together. Each corner held a category of Jews. The first category was composed of those families in which either a single member was associated with the Judenrat, or all of its members were considered vital to the war effort or German economy. The second group was made up of young people who did not have specific jobs that put them in the first group but were able to work productively. The third group was made up of families in which some members had jobs but others did not, like small children or the elderly. Finally, the fourth group was composed of those who were left: the elderly, unemployed, and others deemed by the Nazis to be worthless.

It was early afternoon by the time my family's turn came. All five of us stepped forward and placed our identification papers on the narrow table. My brothers stood up tall, almost like miniature men, appearing unafraid. Lindner raised his left hand with his thumb extended and motioned behind him to his left. We quickly retrieved our papers, which did not receive any new stamp at that point, and walked to our designated corner, with the first group. It was obvious that we were lucky to be in our group, and we were all relieved.

"I'm proud of you guys," I told my brothers.

It was true. I was proud. They worked hard in the factory every day and stood up tall when they faced Lindner and his cronies. They were wise, hardworking, and strong beyond their years. If they hadn't worked and appeared older and stronger than they were that day, we may not have ended up in this corner.

Aaron looked up at me, his eyes smiling.

"I hope we can go home soon," he said.

"Me too."

Our group was to be sent home after our documents were stamped. The second group was to be sent to labor camps, and the members of the third group went through a second heart-wrenching selection in which some of its families were torn apart and divided among the other groups. Those in the fourth group (and whoever remained in the third) were destined for Auschwitz in short order.

I stood with my family, watching the line of those who had yet to be assigned a group. I watched Lindner raise his hand when Genia and her parents approached. This time, he gestured with his pointer finger. They were in the fourth group.

Now it was my turn to panic.

"Kalman, what are you going to do?" It was my mother. It was the first time I heard her speak all day.

"I don't know, Mother. Maybe we can find someone to get them out."

"Do something, Kalman," she said as she squeezed my hand. I think she was giving me permission to put myself in danger, knowing how she would suffer if something were to happen to me. She was telling me to do whatever I could, despite the risks.

I knew there were Jews and Nazis who could be bribed to switch a designation, but we had nothing valuable with us. The Ecksteins still had jewelry hidden but I was afraid to leave the arena to retrieve it. I did not know if I would be able to get back in, or if they would still be here if I did.

I saw some of my old friends, who were also sent to the first group, standing nearby. I left my family and approached them, looking for help. None of them had anything to offer. As I looked around the arena, thinking about what to do next, I saw Genia walk away from her parents in my direction. I knew she was strong, but I was still shocked at her nerve. Maybe she was even more like her brothers than I knew.

I watched Genia take off her coat as she strode toward me and drop it to the ground. A few steps later, she bent down and picked up another coat, a blue one I did not recognize, and buttoned up its wooden toggles to the neckline. She walked past several Nazis, with purpose, like she was not doing anything wrong and just had important matters to attend to on the opposite side of the arena. I stared, in awe.

And then, when she was more than halfway toward my corner, a Jewish policeman grabbed her by the arm. She was past the Gestapo but stopped by a fellow Jew. I wanted to vomit. I knew him from before the war. We were not friends, but he had always seemed like a nice person, and he was from a well-respected Jewish family. I did not have time to think at that moment, but I later wondered how he ended up a member of the militia and how he was able to look at himself in the mirror.

My friends and I moved immediately. We walked quickly towards Genia, fast enough to get there in seconds but not too fast so that we aroused suspicion. Without a word, three of them stood directly in front of the Jewish officer, placing themselves between him and the Gestapo soldiers, so that the Nazis could not see him. Hidden from the Nazis' view, I stepped behind the Jewish officer and as I took his fingers off Genia's arm with my left hand, I punched him hard in the back with my right hand. He lost his footing for a moment, and Genia quickly slipped out of the blue coat, dropped it at his feet, and followed my friends and me to our corner of the arena. He did not follow us or alert the Gestapo. I do not know why. Maybe a bout of conscience. After the war, I heard he died in Auschwitz.

Neither of us spoke as we walked to my assigned corner, where we sat down next to my parents and brothers. Genia looked like she had been hit by a ton of bricks.

"We must get them out. We know where that group is headed," she said.

"We will," I promised, as I took her hand. But how?

It was nearing dusk when the Jewish militia began to round up our group. We lined up once again, and our papers were stamped by a low-ranking SS officer as we exited the arena and walked toward home. The skies suddenly opened and all the moisture that made the day's humidity unbearable poured down. The Ecksteins and thousands of others were standing in the open-air arena in a storm.

My parents and brothers went home and Genia and I ran through the rain toward her apartment to find something we could use to get her parents home. We were almost at her building when we saw her uncle racing towards us carrying coats.

"Bring these to the arena," he said, as he handed me a pile of coats. "Give two of them to Yitzchak and Shprinza and the rest to whoever else may be in need."

Genia and I turned around and ran together back to the arena. We planned to leave the coats, go back to the Ecksteins' apartment, and find some valuables and then someone to bribe. We were absolutely drenched by the time we got to the gates. A Jewish policeman was guarding the entrance and would not let us pass. We explained that we would just drop off the coats and leave. We begged, but he would not budge.

I've been fortunate today, I thought, as I considered my next move. It was an unquestionably awful day, but my family and Genia were safe for now. I got away with punching a policeman. I reflected upon my luck and prepared myself to get physical with the man guarding the gate.

"Fine," he said suddenly, without explanation.

I do not know what changed his mind. Maybe it was the look in Genia's eyes. I was strong for my size, but I was exhausted and wet and barely five foot seven. Despite the brief spell of bravado inside my head, the guard was definitely not afraid of a fight.

"I promise," Genia spoke up. "We will give my parents these coats and leave. They have been sitting there since this morning. Their clothing must be soaked through."

"I cannot let you in there," he said. "I will do it myself. Give me the coats and point out your parents."

We did not have a choice. Genia was able to find her parents through the gates and point them out to the policeman. He took the pile of coats and turned his back to us, walking quickly into the arena.

Once again, Genia and I ran through rain to her building. I pulled the tile off the hiding place as soon as we got upstairs. Their stash was getting smaller and smaller but I found three thin gold rings. I pulled them out, replaced the tile, and turned to where Genia was standing, dripping.

"Here we go again," I said as we headed back down the staircase and outside.

The rain was letting up and it was just drizzling when we arrived back at the arena. There was a crowd at the entrance. We were not the only ones trying to save relatives or friends from Auschwitz. A chorus of screaming and sobbing came from the mob of men and women at the entrance as they all pushed their way forward closer to the gates. Gestapo soldiers were now on guard; there was not a Jewish policeman in sight. They were swinging batons at the mob. My luck for that day had run out.

I felt helpless as I watched Genia watch the scene. I was standing right next to her, but I knew she felt so alone. First her brothers and now her parents.

"Let's go home," Genia said as she took my hand and turned her back to the gates.

"We can wait. We will stay all night if we have to. We will get your parents out."

"You know it is impossible. There is nothing to be done. If we stay here past curfew we will be forced to join them on the other side of the gates."

She dropped my hand and left me behind as she walked away from the arena. I had never felt more torn. Genia seemed to have accepted that her parents were headed for a death camp. As well as I knew her, I could not begin to imagine what was going through her head, but I would not accept that we could not prevent or at least delay her parents' fate. We were so very different that way. As much as I loved her, I knew that Genia was a glass-half-empty kind of person. And I always saw the glass as half full. She lost hope for her parents and maybe even for herself that day, but I never lost hope. I prayed that we could save her parents, and that one day this would all be over.

CHAPTER 13

THERE WAS NOTHING to be done at the gate, so I thought about my next steps as I walked back toward the center of town. I knew there must be someone who could help. I hadn't seen my childhood friend Eli for over a year, but his older brother worked for the Judenrat. It was a long shot, but the only idea I had at the moment. I told myself not to judge him as I walked to their apartment, three thin gold rings still in my pocket.

I knocked on the door and waited for what seemed like a very long time for it to open.

The Judenrat employee himself, Eli's brother, opened the door and shut it behind him as he stepped out to the building's hallway.

"Kalman," he said. "I have not seen you in a while. Eli is not home. He should be back any minute. Curfew begins soon."

"I am not looking for Eli. I am looking for you. I am desperate for your help. I am not sure if you know my girlfriend, Genia Eckstein, but her family is in trouble and I can't think of anywhere else to go."

"I know her brothers. Are they back? Those guys are trouble incarnate."

"It's not them. We still haven't heard anything from them. It's her parents. They were relegated to the fourth group at the arena today. We all know what awaits them. With her brothers gone, if I can't get Genia's parents out of that arena, she will be left with no family. Please help me."

"Go home," he said, with a straight face as he began to shut the door in mine.

I had no idea whether he was sending me home because he was saying no to my plea for help or so that he could go save the Ecksteins.

I held the rings inside my pocket, not sure what to do with them. There were some guys who were slick enough to hand over jewelry in a bribe. Not me! I was an amateur in the world of bribery and had not prepared myself for the actual payoff. My mind was racing. I could hear my heart beating and feel perspiration wetting my shirt. Do I just pull them out and hand them over? Do I ask him first if he plans to help? I stood there for a moment, holding the door open and trying to figure it all out.

"Kalman," he said, smiling this time. "Relax. Just go home."

I turned with the rings still in my pocket and left. I assumed he meant for me to wait for him at my home. I walked straight home to find my parents and brothers all sitting at the table waiting anxiously. My father stood up and paced the room with me as I updated them on my attempt to save the Ecksteins.

"So Genia is home alone?" my mother asked when I finished.

"I think so. Eli's brother told me to come home and wait. I think he is going to find me here. I cannot go to Genia's in case he will come here, and I miss him."

"You're right," she said. And I joined them at the table.

My brothers went to sleep shortly thereafter, and my parents and I sat at that table for over two hours. It was well past curfew when we heard voices outside the door. I jumped up and opened the door, thrilled to see the Ecksteins standing there with my new Judenrat friend. In my relief, I forgot about the need to be slick. I reached into my pocket and handed him the three rings. I really do not believe he helped me only for a reward; he helped because he was a kind person trying to do a good thing. Maybe not all Jews who joined the militia were bad people. He deserved compensation nonetheless, perhaps even more so.

He shook my hand and left, leaving the Ecksteins standing in the doorway. They looked terrible, not just elderly, but truly old. They were so frail and thin; I did not know how they made it from the arena to our home. I ushered them inside to the table and my mother heated water for tea as my father wrapped blankets around their shoulders. Mrs. Eckstein appeared to slowly gain some strength as she warmed up, a bit of color returning to her face. Mr. Eckstein did not. I was afraid for him, and I could tell my parents were too.

The best course of action seemed to be to get him home and into bed. Maybe he would be better in the morning. Slowly, the Ecksteins and I made our way to their apartment. I walked between them, holding on to each of their elbows, not even thinking about violating curfew. My only thought was that I must get Mr. Eckstein home before he collapsed.

Thankfully, we arrived at the Ecksteins' apartment without incident, and after a precarious trip up the stairs and a quick knock, Genia met us at the door. She hugged her parents with so much force that she almost knocked them down. Then she looked at me with surprisingly dry eyes, and silently thanked me. Neither of us had to say a word.

"Let's get your father to bed, Genia," Mrs. Eckstein spoke first.

"Yes, and you too Mother," Genia responded.

I busied myself filling the kettle while Genia helped her parents settle in. She met me in the kitchen when they were in bed. I was expecting tears but none came. I could not remember the last time I saw her cry. Maybe she was simply out of tears.

"We need to get married, Kalman," she said, as we stood side by side, both leaning against the counter.

"What makes you say that now?" I asked, turning to look at her. We knew we would marry at some point, but it had been over a year since we last discussed it. This hardly seemed the time.

"It's too dangerous," I told her. "And why now? I don't want to build a home in this environment. Let's wait until this is all over, after the war, when your brothers and Julia come home. Let's wait until we can truly celebrate."

"This will never be over," Genia said. "Even if the war ends one day and by some miracle you and I are still alive, our parents will not survive this war. I am profoundly grateful to have my parents home tonight, but you cannot honestly believe that either of our parents, especially mine, can weather much more suffering. There will come a time when we won't be able to save them, or maybe even save ourselves, from those trains and beyond."

"And how would getting married help?"

"It won't. But it will give them joy. And if we are going to lose them soon, be it next month, or next year, let's give them a little bit of joy in all of their suffering."

"Jews! Jews! Open the door!"

I was just about to agree with Genia when the shouting began. The SS was yelling again. Always so loud. I opened the door, my first worry being that they would ask for identification. My papers still listed my aunt's home address, and I was not supposed to be anywhere else after curfew. But they stormed past me, leading to my second and larger worry. Someone found out the Ecksteins left the arena, and they were here to take them back. They walked in and out of rooms with Genia and me following closely behind. When we all entered the Ecksteins' bedroom, they both jumped out of bed, terrified.

"All of you leave this apartment now," one of the officers commanded.

"Where are you taking us?" Mr. Eckstein asked, his voice shaking. I had not heard him speak since he arrived at my apartment from the arena.

"We are not taking you anywhere. Find somewhere else to go. You have ten minutes. This entire building will be vacated for the next twenty-four hours. You may return the day after tomorrow."

The Ecksteins got dressed and packed a small bag. There was no time to remove the tile and take the little valuable jewelry that remained. It was almost morning, and I was exhausted as we left the building with all the other residents. Without a discussion, the four of us walked to my home.

My family was sleeping when we arrived. The Ecksteins went straight to bed in Julia's room, Genia quickly fell asleep on the sofa, and I think I was sleeping before my head hit the pillow in the room I shared with my brothers. It had been such a long day. And who knew what tomorrow would bring.

CHAPTER 14

T HE NEXT MORNING brought more bad news. Thousands of Jews had spent the night on the wet ground of the arena, awaiting their fate. In the early morning hours, they were marched into town, where they were forced into several large apartment buildings that had been cleared of occupants. The Ecksteins' building was one of those.

The buildings were locked and guarded. There was no food, aside from the small amounts thrown in through windows by family members and other sympathetic Jews. There was virtually no way out. A small number were smuggled out after relatives paid exorbitant bribes to the Judenrat. Rumor had it that a handful of Jews escaped by digging a tunnel into the basement of another building, but that was quickly discovered and sealed. Some, to avoid dying at the hands of the Nazis, jumped off the buildings' roofs and out of windows, taking their own lives.

After two days, guards began marching those locked inside to the train station, forcing them into cattle cars. It took another three days for the Nazis to empty the buildings and send the thousands of Jews who were inside to Auschwitz. Those of us left behind had to clean up the mess.

And it was a literal mess. The day after the buildings were emptied, Genia and I met at her apartment after work to plan for the Ecksteins' return. The Judenrat had sent workers to clean the building's common areas, and they were just getting started when we arrived. I had never seen or smelled anything like it. We were overcome by the odor before we stepped inside the building. We covered our faces with our sleeves and walked up the stairs. The entire building smelled like a barn. We saw feces and vomit along the stairwell.

The Ecksteins' apartment fared no better. The stench was awful and the view the same. While by some miracle, no one had found the hiding place behind the tile, their pristine home was destroyed by a helpless, terrified mob, lacking sufficient food, water, and facilities. Nothing was spared.

We had to clean the apartment before we brought Genia's parents back home. The first thing I did was open all of the windows. There was no way that place would be habitable again without being aired out. And then, we scrubbed everything – furniture, walls, floors, pots and pans, kitchen utensils, clothing. Soap was expensive on the black market, and while we did get some, we had to use it sparingly. It took almost a week of open windows and cleaning every day after work to make the apartment livable again.

It was worth every minute. I caught a glimpse of the Ecksteins' old selves as I watched them walk into their home, standing taller and prouder than I had seen in ages. But it was only fleeting. If the suffering I saw at the soccer arena and at the Ecksteins' building taught me anything, it was that our lives were not returning to normal anytime soon. They were going to get worse. Genia was right after the selection at the soccer arena. We had to get married, and soon, or our parents would never see it happen.

Our engagement lasted ten days. There was no time to spare. Any one of us could have been taken away at any time. It was illegal for Jews to get married under Nazi rule, but we wanted to give our parents one day to remember in the midst of their misery, as what we had come to believe to be inevitable approached.

On August 30, 1942, we were married at the Ecksteins' home. Someone – I never found out who – bought meat, ingredients for a cake, and even liquor, on the black market. I wore a navy blue suit and Genia wore a light blue dress. She was beautiful.

We had a brief ceremony and then a truly festive meal despite the terrible world outside. The table was set with the Ecksteins' monogrammed linens and formal china, which I was shocked to see for the first time in years. The stemware was crystal and serving pieces were silver, all of which I had assumed were stolen by Nazis or sold at some point in the last several years. I do not know where they hid it all, certainly not behind the tile in the kitchen. It was like a dream.

Until banging on the door woke me up. The dining room fell silent. We all sat frozen for what felt like several minutes but was probably just a few seconds. Then came more banging, this time followed by shouts to open the door. I motioned to Aaron, and he opened the door. Two Gestapo officers marched into the dining room. We knew that discovery was a possibility when we planned to marry but I could not believe it actually happened. Maybe our parents would have been better off without this day. I looked around the table. Everyone I loved was in danger. It was my fault. I was terrified, and in that moment, so very sorry.

It must have been obvious to them that we were celebrating a wedding. Or maybe someone tipped them off.

"Who is the groom?" one of the officers asked as he pulled his gun from the holster.

I stood.

"I am the groom."

I answered in German. I looked straight at him as I spoke. He was a tall man, muscular, with blonde, almost white hair under his hat, and bright blue eyes. He was a walking Nazi advertisement for the superior Aryan race.

He raised his gun and pointed it at me. I closed my eyes and thought I was about to die. I said the Shema[10] under my breath.

"Hear O' Israel. The Lord is our God. The Lord is One."

My mother gasped loudly, and as the Nazi turned to look in her direction, I heard my cousin Hanna's voice.

"Hans! Hans! Don't shoot. Hans! He is my brother," she said. All eyes turned to Hanna. Then back to the Nazi named Hans. He lowered his gun, and I took a breath. Hanna jumped out of her seat, ran to where Hans stood, and hugged him. Hugged him! Now it was Hans's turn to freeze. He did not return her embrace. He was being hugged by a Jew while standing in the center of an illegal wedding celebration.

---

10. The Shema prayer is traditionally recited twice a day, morning and evening. Jews who fear for their lives may also say the Shema, seeking protection from God.

But Hanna had always had a way with men. She ignored his temporary paralysis, took his hand in one of hers, grabbed a bottle of liquor in the other, and dragged him out of the dining room. The other Nazi followed.

Hanna saved my life and probably the lives of everyone at the wedding. She got two Gestapo officers drunk in a bedroom as we finished our meal. And despite the scare, it was truly a joyous day, pure happiness amid a living hell.

CHAPTER 15

I MOVED IN WITH Genia and her parents on the day of our
wedding. We lived in their home for two months before we
were all sent to the ghetto. The Nazis established two ghettos
in Sosnowiec; the larger one was in the Srodula district and the
other, Stary Sosnowiec, was on the other side of the city. By the
time the ghettos were completed in late winter 1943, there were
approximately 15,000 people in the larger ghetto and 5,000 in the
smaller one.

My parents, brothers, Genia, and I were assigned to the Srodula
ghetto. The smaller ghetto, to which Genia's parents had been
assigned, was clearly meant for those who would not be of much use
to the Nazis. We assumed that its residents would be the first to be
deported and sent to death.

We had to save them. Genia and I debated whether we were
better off quietly taking them with us instead of trying to get them
officially moved. Still for the most part a rule-follower, I wanted their
move to be official. I was afraid of the repercussions if we did not
follow the Judenrat's housing assignment. Genia was generally more
willing to break the rules and was also afraid of what would happen
if we were unable to make the change. We decided to try to take the
official route, and if we failed, to take them with us anyway. Formal
recognition would bring with it nominal food rations, which were
better than no food rations.

I emptied the stash behind the Ecksteins' tile and brought what
was left – mostly small pieces of silver – to the Judenrat office. Just
a few months after my introduction to bribery, I walked confidently

into the crowded Judenrat office, placed the silver on the first desk that I saw, and spoke to the woman sitting at that desk.

"I need my in-laws switched to the Srodula ghetto," I said as she eyed the silver.

"What are their names?" she asked, the pile of silver sitting out in the open on her desk.

"Eckstein, Yitchak and Shprinza."

"Take this home with you. Please be sure to tear up the card indicating that they belong in Stary Sosnowiec. There is no space for additional families in Srodula so I cannot assign them a home. You will share your home with them."

She handed me a card assigning them to Srodula. Then she walked over to a shelf ten feet away, from which she removed a large book. She came back to her desk, opened the book, and wrote something on the last page. She closed the book, stood up again, returned the book to its shelf, and sat down when she returned to her desk. Only then did she place the silver in her drawer. I took the card and walked out, shaking my head. I was not naive as to how the Judenrat functioned; what I found shocking was the shamelessness. How long would that silver have sat on a desk before someone batted an eye? I still had a lot to learn.

CHAPTER 16

T HE JUDENRAT WAS responsible for transferring Jews from their homes to the ghettos. We were sent to live in the Srodula district, the poorest, most dilapidated area of Sosnowiec, while its former Polish residents moved into our now vacated homes in middle class and wealthy neighborhoods. We were assigned to a two-room apartment consisting of a kitchen and a living room. The Luzens, a young family with two small boys, aged 6 and 8, lived in the kitchen, while the eight of us – my parents, my brothers, the Ecksteins, Genia and I – shared the living room. There were no indoor bathroom facilities or running water. We tried to provide privacy by hanging sheets throughout the apartment. We were forced to share a single outhouse with the inhabitants of the entire building. The outhouse and water pump in Lvov were luxurious in comparison.

Living conditions in the ghetto were awful, but whatever its flaws, the Judenrat did attempt to help the Jewish community from its new office inside the ghetto. The Judenrat set up an orphanage, reopened soup kitchens, and kept a hospital running. There were a handful of Jewish shops, which accepted specially printed money with no value outside the ghetto. There were no fences surrounding the ghetto, but aside from daily marches to and from work under guard, we were not permitted to leave. Anyway, there was nowhere to go. We heard stories about Jews who ran away and hid in forests in other parts of Poland, but there were no forests near Sosnowiec. Our hideouts were limited to places inside the ghetto where we could stay for only short periods of time. Some parents, like the ones we shared our apartment with, built false ceilings so that their children could hide when people were being rounded up and sent on trains.

Cellars were another popular hiding place in Srodula. Each day, before Genia and I went to work, we hid her parents in the cellar with a bottle of water, a piece of bread, and an empty bucket, locking them in and covering the entrance with a large wicker crate. We were afraid that because they were unemployed, they would be the first sent away. And we learned more every day about what that meant. We were fewer than forty kilometers from Auschwitz. If the Ecksteins were put on a train while we were at work, we would never see them again.

Individual Jews disappeared from the ghetto, randomly dragged off the street and thrown onto the back of trucks or shot in the middle of the street for no apparent reason. Parents returned from work to find their children gone. But there was no large-scale organized deportation from the ghetto for the first few months.

That changed in the spring of 1943. My father and I were both working at the furniture factory where I had worked before I went to Annaburg. The SS no longer needed us to renovate their offices, so we were both assigned jobs at the factory when we moved to the ghetto. I cut my arm on a piece of machinery in March of 1943 and was at the Jewish hospital getting my bandage changed when I heard rumblings.

Apparently, two members of the Judenrat had arrived that morning and removed their family members from the hospital despite doctors' objections. The chatty Jewish nurse bandaging my arm was sure that those in the hospital would be deported shortly. She was hoping to go home soon so that she did not have to witness the scene. She had been there when the Jewish militia emptied out the old Jewish hospital in Sosnowiec, the one outside the ghetto, and could not imagine watching it again. She had a bad feeling about this one, she told me.

Then I felt uneasy. As I walked out of the hospital, everything seemed off. The ghetto streets were even more chaotic than usual and the number of Jewish policemen seemed to have doubled. I ran the few blocks home and told my parents that trouble was brewing. I took a loaf of bread and a pitcher of water and led my parents and in-laws into the cellar. I locked them in, covered the entrance with our wicker trunk, and hoped for the best.

That evening, the Gestapo surrounded the ghetto with flood lights.

The Jewish militia used loudspeakers to announce that all residents of the ghetto were to appear at the central square. Gestapo soldiers stood guard at the Ghetto entrance, preventing any exit.

I walked over to the square just as Genia and my brothers were arriving there from work. We stood in line for hours waiting for our identification papers to be checked before the Jewish militia sent us home. It seemed that everyone who assembled at the square and presented proper identification was permitted to remain in the ghetto, while those who did not have appropriate documentation were taken immediately to a transit camp, and from there to the train station. Thankfully, our parents remained in the cellar where I left them; once again, our family managed to remain united.

Our apartment-mates did not seem so lucky that night. Mr. and Mrs. Luzen went straight to the square after work. Their children, as far as they knew, were hidden in the apartment's false ceiling all day. But when they arrived at home from the square and pulled open the false ceiling, their boys were missing. They panicked. Genia and I joined them in their search for their sons. We checked the cellar and knocked on all of the building's doors asking if anyone had seen the boys. No one knew anything.

Just as we finished looking around the building and entered our apartment, Genia and I heard sounds of a joyful reunion coming from outside. They found their sons! The boys were afraid they would be discovered when they heard the call for all the Jews to come to the square. They went to the outhouse and lowered themselves into the hole, where they waited, sitting on carrying beams, until they heard their parents call their names.

I watched the boys and their parents walk into the apartment smiling, but smelling of an outhouse and covered in human excrement. I understood the parents' pride in their boys' resourcefulness and the family's profound joy. But for me, that evening brought a new low. There is nothing acceptable about small children, afraid for their lives, hiding in outhouse holes. It was the newest tragedy in our tragic world.

CHAPTER 17

AFTER THE ROUND up in March, the Judenrat posted almost daily lists of people who were to report to the transit camp – and from there to the train station – with little notice. From the train station, they would be sent on to labor or death camps. We lived in fear, waiting to be separated. In June, our nightmare came true.

We heard a knock on the door shortly after curfew one night in mid-June. It was a pleasant night, and we were sitting on the floor playing cards, a breeze coming through the open window. I stood and went to the door.

"Kalman and Genia Sztajer," said the Jewish militiaman, looking at his shoes as he handed me a piece of paper. I took some comfort in the fact that he could not bear to look at me.

"Kalman, what is it?" Genia asked as she rose and came to meet me at the door.

"This will be posted tomorrow morning as you go to work. Report to the square after work tomorrow, or there will be consequences," said the militiaman, still looking down.

Genia and I stood in front of the open door as he turned and walked away. He had handed me a list, like the ones that were being posted throughout the ghetto on a regular basis. We had seen so many families torn apart, and now it was our turn. The paper read "Couples Transport," and I recognized some of the names listed, young married couples like us. I do not know how our illegal marriage was reported or why we were given advance notice of the transport, but I was grateful that it gave us an opportunity to say goodbye, and for our parents to know that wherever Genia and I were going, it would be together.

None of us slept that night. Genia and I laid awake worrying about how our parents would fare without us – we knew not well. And our parents, as much as our roles had been reversed the past couple of years, were still parents – parents who knew that they had less than a day before they would lose their children, likely forever.

After what seemed like a never-ending night, we said our final goodbyes to the Ecksteins as we closed the cellar door behind them before we went to work. Genia and I heard their cries as we each walked toward our group of co-workers waiting in the square to be marched to work.

I was sweating as soon as we began to walk, having worn several layers of clothing and a pair of warm boots in preparation for wherever I was going. It was always wise to dress warmly for a deportation; you never knew how long you would be gone or how cold it would be. I met my workmates from the furniture factory, including my father, and marched to work as usual. The same list we had received the previous evening was posted on walls throughout the ghetto. Otherwise, it was a typical day in my new normal. I noticed my father look at me from across the factory floor several times, but I avoided all eye contact. I kept my eyes on the wooden dresser I was sanding, determined not to cry.

At the end of the workday, I walked back to the ghetto next to my father. He stuck a roll in my coat pocket just as we left the factory. We walked without speaking because we were forced to, as usual, but I appreciated the forced silence because there was nothing to say. I could not say goodbye.

The SS guards who marched us back and forth to work each day began to yell as we entered the ghetto.

"Straight to the square, Jews! Do not stop! If you are on the list, go directly to the square!"

My father squeezed my arm. I still could not look at him. Our SS escorts usually stopped at the ghetto entrance while the Jewish militia policed inside the ghetto. For the first time, the SS guards entered the ghetto along with us. I clenched my jaw and looked down. I watched the shoes of the man in front of me. They were dirty, but the soles looked new. Thick pieces of brown rubber hit the pavement lightly, and I wondered how he got so lucky.

We arrived to chaos in the square. My father spotted my mother, brothers, and Genia standing together, and the two of us scrambled through the crowd to reach them. The Ecksteins were still hidden in the cellar, waiting for someone to unlock the door.

I barely had a chance to greet my family before our names were called. My mother became hysterical, but I held my own hysteria inside. It was my last chance to be strong for my parents and my brothers. I hugged them all silently, afraid that if I spoke, I too would break down. My father sent my brothers to get the Ecksteins out of the cellar. I watched the backs of their heads as they walked away. Then I stood frozen in place, as Genia stepped back, leaving me with my parents.

It turned out my father was the strong one. He was able to speak. For the second time in as many years, he blessed a child knowing that it was likely for the last time. He placed both of his hands on my head as he whispered his weekly blessing into my ear.

"May God make you like Ephraim and Menashe. May God bless you and protect you. May God shine His face on you and be gracious to you. May God turn His face to you and grant you peace."[11]

He removed his trembling hands from my head and gently nudged my mother away from me. She stood between us, holding my left hand as he pulled her, more forcefully now. I felt something wet hit me in the back of the neck and my mother suddenly let go. The Nazis sprayed my parents and the others remaining in the ghetto with fire hoses until they ran away or fell. My mother dropped my hand as she collapsed, alongside my father, both of them on the ground, wet and crying. That was the last time I saw them.

I closed my eyes tightly to stop the tears. When I opened them I turned and walked toward Genia. We followed the crowd to the train station.

---

11. Nachum recited the priestly blessing traditionally bestowed upon sons each Shabbat.

CHAPTER 18

G ENIA AND I were sent to Annaburg. It was the same camp I had been at two years before, but bigger now, having been expanded to include more barracks as well as workshops for trades. The original camp was being used as a headquarters for Nazis responsible for ghetto liquidations and labor camps.

We arrived at night, as was customary for camp arrivals. The Nazis knew it was scarier at night, and the more frightened we were, the greater their control. Bright lights hit us as soon as we stepped off the train, a boxcar train this time, and the yelling began.

"Off Jews! Off Jews!"

"Men to the left. Women to the right. Men to the left. Women to the right."

"Line up in an orderly fashion and take a bar of soap as you pass the barrel. You will be going straight to the showers. Leave your clothing outside. It will be disinfected, and you may reclaim it after you've showered."

I squeezed Genia's hand as we separated, and I followed the men to the left.

This is it, I thought to myself. The rumors were true. They're going to gas us in the showers. After all I had been through, it was still hard to believe. I was reminded of a young boy who appeared in the ghetto one day shortly after we moved there. He looked about my brother Aaron's age. He told whoever would listen that he had escaped from Auschwitz, and that in Auschwitz, Jews were being gassed to death in showers, their bodies burned to ash in crematoriums. He was sent to the mental health floor of the ghetto's Jewish hospital, deemed insane.

He did not seem crazy now, I thought, as I took a bar of soap and undressed out of my layers. I walked slowly into the room of shower heads. Water was flowing! No gas! There were showers! I broke into a smile as I lathered my body with soap and walked under a stream of freezing water. Then it was burning hot, then freezing cold, then burning hot, and so on and so on, switching between hot and cold. But I did not care. I was alive, and even clean.

"Out! Out! Jews! Quickly find your clothes and get dressed!"

We had only been in the showers for a few minutes. Our clothing was all gathered into one large wet pile just outside the showers. I think they used some sort of liquid disinfectant, but had not had time to dry the clothing. We dressed in our wet clothing and went outside. I was wearing three layers of wet clothing, and it was heavy. I was so happy to be alive, I did not care. Maybe I would have felt differently if it were January.

The thirty men in our transport were ordered to form a single line. As we waited in line, tired and wet, we saw the women lining up on the opposite side of the fence. I watched Genia find a place in line, happy to see that she too was given an actual shower. We were both alive.

The women were quickly marched away on their side of the fence, while I followed my line for a short walk into a barrack. The barrack was lined with wooden bunks, identical to the ones I remembered from my last time at Annaburg. Most of them were already occupied, but there were enough for each of us newcomers to have his own. I found an empty bed, hung my wet clothing over the side to dry, and fell asleep in my still damp underclothes.

I was woken up early by a chatty Czechoslovakian who had been asleep in the bunk beneath mine when I arrived the night before. He filled me in on the details of Annaburg in its current iteration. We were approximately three hundred inmates, more men than women, tasked with working for the German war machine. The Nazis knew exactly who we all were and our value to their system before they brought us here. We were all experienced in our trades – builders, tailors, shoemakers, goldsmiths, and even a diamond setter.

The tailors made underwear out of prayer shawls stolen from Jews for German soldiers, clothing for Nazi officers, and sometimes dresses for the prostitutes those officers invited to their quarters in Annaburg. The goldsmiths and diamond setters maintained and repurposed jewelry looted from Nazi victims, sometimes for the officers and their families, and sometimes for the very same prostitutes. The shoemakers worked on Nazi boots, the sound of which terrified so many victims, and oversaw production of wooden clogs by a group of the unskilled wives brought along in our transport.

We were permitted to wear our own shoes and clothing at Annaburg, as long as a yellow star was visible at all times, although we had the option of wearing striped uniforms, which some Jews wore as an extra layer for warmth. The clogs were for Jewish inmates of other camps. They expedited death, particularly on long marches in the winter. If you slowed down on a march because your clogs were heavy, or covered in snow, you would be shot for slowing down, and if you bent down to clear off the snow accumulating on your clogs, you would be shot for bending down. Either way, clogs led to death.

I acclimated quickly to Annaburg. I was tasked with building workshops for the various trades. I took apart old barracks and used the wood to build whatever was needed for each of the trades, made repairs, and sometimes built small pieces of furniture for the Nazi officers.

Genia was the housekeeper for General Ulver, one of the higher-ups at Annaburg. He picked her out of the line of women that first night, and he told her in no uncertain terms that if he found a crease in a single shirt hanging in his closet or on any of his bed linens, he would shoot her on the spot. He insisted that she clean his Persian rug daily, so she carried it outside on her back and beat it first thing each morning. He also relieved himself in a chamber pot rather than in the toilet attached to his bedroom, simply so that Genia would be forced to empty his waste and clean the pot.

The prisoners at Annaburg formed a sort of civilized community. We were a small group, so we all knew each other, and we worked together to survive. We shared the little bits of food we came across and helped each other complete work. At Annaburg, we were hungry, but clean. We were provided a small portion of bread and a thin cup of soup daily. But we were often in close contact with Nazi officers who were afraid that we would pass lice or disease along to them, so we were permitted to shower regularly, with real soap. When we weren't working, Genia and I were able to see each other through the fence that separated the genders. Sometimes she brought bits of food that the women who worked in the kitchen shared.

Over the approximately year and a half we were in Annaburg, there were periodic transports from Annaburg to Auschwitz, mostly of those who were sick, or whose services were no longer needed. By late 1944, there were only eighty prisoners remaining; Genia and I were among them.

Our rations were getting smaller and we were all getting weaker. One evening, feeling faint, I sat on a railing outside the kitchen to drink my soup. The head kapo,[12] who I knew from Sosnowiec, approached me.

"Kalman," he said, "tomorrow when you go out to work with the other men, I'd like for you to be kapo. Hersh was taken away today, and you'll take his place."

"Thank you," I responded. I stood without finishing my soup and continued.

"But no thank you. I have no choice but to be here. I have no choice but to work. But I will choose to work as a plain Jew. And if I die here, or elsewhere at the hands of the Nazis, I will die as a plain Jew. I will not be a kapo to save myself. If I live through this war, I'll have to live with myself after the war."

I watched him walk away without a response and sat on the railing wondering if I had made a mistake. I knew it wasn't a mistake to refuse the position of kapo. I wanted to live, but not at the expense of another Jew. Maybe I should have held my tongue though, and not sounded so judgmental. As kapo he had a fair amount of control over me.

---

12. A kapo, or *Funktionshäftling*, was a prisoner in a Nazi camp assigned by SS guards to assist with administrative tasks or to supervise prisoners.

CHAPTER 19

I LOOKED OVER MY shoulder for a couple of days, but nothing came of that conversation. Not long after, no Jew's position in Annaburg could save him or her. On December 24, 1944, my twenty-fourth birthday, the guards gathered all the prisoners into one group, men and women together, and surrounded us. It was cold and windy, with a light snow falling. They told us it was time to leave the camp, and we began our march, followed by two trucks carrying the Nazi officers' personal effects, furniture, clothing, artwork, and other items they had stolen from Jews.

"You see, Kalman," Genia said as soon as we passed through the gates, "there is no God. No God would have sent this weather for a march."

"God is sending this weather for the Russians," I told her. "The Germans don't fight as well as the Russians do in inclement weather. The worse the weather, the quicker the Russians will advance, and this will all be over."

Genia laughed. I knew she would laugh at me before I even spoke. She was adamant that no God could allow such death and suffering among Europe's Jews, and thought I was foolish for continuing to believe. Genia had never been particularly religious, but she lost all faith about two months after we arrived in Annaburg. In August 1943, one of her second cousins arrived in Annaburg as part of a very small transport, not more than thirty Jews in total. She told Genia about the liquidation of the Srodula ghetto and the transport of our families to Auschwitz. We did not find out for certain until after the war that the entire transport was sent directly to the gas chambers, but we knew there was no way our parents could have survived Auschwitz. Genia lost what little faith she had with news of her parents' fate.

My faith in God may have been foolish. I doubted it myself at points during the war years. But something inside made me continue to believe and to hope, even as we marched on in the snow. We did not know where we were going, but we overheard enough to know that we were heading away from the Russian front.

The Nazi guards were more lax than I had ever seen. There was no yelling at all. I assumed that meant they knew the end was near.

"Do you see how they're not yelling?" I asked Genia, a full night and day into our march. "I bet they know this is the end. They're not so in control anymore."

"For us, it's the end. Why would they keep us alive at this point? We're probably marching until we drop, or at least until we reach Auschwitz, where they can kill us with gas. They won't waste bullets on those of us left."

"Please, Genia, try to have some hope. I know it feels like everything is lost, but we still have each other. I cannot make you believe, or make you hope. That's yours to do alone. But I can't just give up. I will continue to believe and hope enough for both of us for as long as I may live."

Genia did not answer. She thought I was foolish, that I could not accept the reality unfolding around us. We did not speak about anything of consequence for the rest of the march.

We marched for almost forty-eight hours in all, stopping to rest for short periods in the snow. I know we needed some breaks, but it was easier to stay warm when we were moving.

Finally, we came to a stop at a train crossing. There was no station, just a boxcar train stopped along the snow-covered tracks. The Nazis loaded the contents of the trucks into one of the boxcars and directed us into another one.

CHAPTER 20

"**O**UT! OUT, JEWS!"
There was the yelling again. I must have fallen asleep standing upright in the crowded boxcar and woke to yelling. It was dark outside as we exited the train. There were no flood lights shining on us, just flashlights held by the guards barking orders.

A prisoner dressed in a striped uniform pushed a wheelbarrow on the other end of the train platform. It was hard to see in the dark, but it looked like there was meat inside. When was the last time I had meat? I could not believe my eyes. I was right to hope, I thought; we are going to be okay. Late night arrival at a new concentration camp was not the time for "I told you so's," so I showed Genia the meat without commentary.

"Look, Genia, to your left. Can you see it? There's meat at this camp."

We watched the man and his meat as he came closer. And then he came too close. Close enough for us to see inside the wheelbarrow. Human remains. It was wise to leave out the commentary. Genia's "I told you so" came in the form of a look I would never forget – a look of utter hopelessness.

Once again, we were separated, with a swift "men to the right, women to the left," and I followed the line of men. We were told to disrobe because we would be going into the showers. I figured there was a fifty-fifty chance I would walk straight into a gas chamber, but I hoped this place was more like Annaburg than it appeared.

"Where can I leave my photos?" I asked a kapo supervising the process. I still had ten photos of my family that I was able to hold on to at Annaburg and I did not want to lose them.

"Welcome to Gross-Rosen," he said. "You won't need photos here."

He spoke German in an unfamiliar accent. Now, even I thought that fifty-fifty was optimistic. I put the photos inside my boots and left those, along with my clothing, in the growing pile of clothing and shoes. I walked through a long tunnel to reach the showers, which thankfully, were actual showers. They were freezing showers, but any water was better than gas.

When we got out of the showers, we waited, naked and cold, to be shaved. When it was my turn, I stood with my arms raised straight up above my head as a prisoner shaved my entire body. Then we were directed, one at a time, to a barrel of disinfectant. I climbed into the barrel and dunked by head, as instructed. The burning was awful. My skin was on fire. I thought my eyes would never stop stinging.

Next, I found myself outside, still naked, standing at the edge of another heap of clothing.

"Get dressed and get in line! Now! Jews! Get dressed and get in line!"

Kapos were yelling, sounding so much like the actual Nazis on whose behalf they operated. I was scared, not only for my own uncertain future, but also of what had already taken place. All kapos, no matter their religion, country of origin, or experiences before the war, began as inmates in concentration camps. It was frightening to see how some of them, many of them in fact, had become more than just messengers for the Nazis. They were watered-down versions of the Nazis themselves.

And I had to obey them. There was no time to pick through the pile and find my own clothing, if it was even there. I lost my boots and photos that night. Naked, wet, and cold, prisoners grabbed whatever clothing they could. I pulled out a pair of too-big shoes, a pair of too-long pants, a shirt that actually fit, and what I think was a woman's coat. At least it was warm. None of it was clean, which made me wonder why they disinfected us. I was dirtier in these clothes than I had been when I arrived.

Dressed in my "new" clothes, I followed the rest of the men onto an open field. Kapos had supervised our entry into Gross-Rosen thus far, but as we walked toward the field, we passed four uniformed Nazis sitting at a long table. They just sat and watched us proceed without a word. There was no arbitrary selection, no separation of families, no yelling, just silent observation of unnaturally skinny men in ill-fitting, mismatched clothing.

Just past the table, I saw two kapos. One of them sat on a lone chair, with an open book in his lap, while the other, bald and bareheaded despite the weather, stood next to the chair holding a stack of cards. I watched him hand one to each man who shuffled by and then take the card back a few seconds later. I wondered what was on the cards; maybe they were work assignments, I thought. It seemed inefficient to assign work without knowing about our skills first, as they did at Annaburg, but I had already learned that Gross-Rosen was not Annaburg. Life worked differently here.

I got my card when it was my turn to pass the kapos.

"Name," said the bald kapo in Russian accented German.

"Kalman Sztajer," I told him.

"Your prisoner number is nine – five – seven – seven – seven," said the seated kapo, as he wrote what I assumed was my name in the notebook on his lap.

The bald one handed me a small square card with a single number printed on it. Nine – five – seven – seven – seven. There was a space between the five and the first seven. I handed the card back to him and repeated my number over and over again in my head, committing it to memory.

I joined the other men, standing in the dark, in three lines, for hours. Four different guards counted us over the course of those hours. I was exhausted and freezing, and my skin still stung. Finally, someone decided it was time for us to move along, and we were sent to the barracks. They were nothing like the barracks at Annaburg. They were unfinished and smelled like mold. There were no bunks. Countless men sat on the ground, leaning on each other, asleep. There was not enough room for them to lay down.

I joined the men on the ground. Despite my exhaustion, I stayed awake all night, my first night at Gross-Rosen. I sat in shock, with hundreds of dirty, hungry, sickly men, on a cold damp floor, and listened to the wind roar outside. Amazingly, and horrifically, I missed Annaburg.

Before dawn, a kapo woke some of the sleeping men by hitting them with a wooden bat. The screams of those prisoners quickly woke the others. Most of the men were unphased, which led me to believe that this was the normal wake-up routine. I followed the crowd out of the barrack to the same field on which we stood the previous evening. Some of the men were too weak or sick to stand up and walk over to the field. Others had died overnight. I stepped around the sick and the dead, still in shock, and found a place in line outside.

We stood for hours. I do not know how many times we were counted. Some men dropped in their places and were left on the cold, wet ground until the counting was done. Suddenly, a guard yelled "finished" and we were done standing in line.

"Where do we go now? I need to get a work assignment," I said to the man who had been standing to my right for the last several hours.

"You must be new here," he said. "There is nowhere to go at Gross-Rosen. And no work. They count us in the morning and again in the evening. In between roll calls, we stand around, or sit around, or for those who are able, walk around. We do nothing but wait."

"Wait for what? For the war to end?" I asked.

He smiled. He was missing several teeth.

"To end up like the guys who don't get counted," he said as he looked over to the barrack. Several prisoners were carrying the bodies of those who did not wake up that morning out of the barrack and placing them in a pile just outside.

I turned away from him. I would not wait to die. I walked around looking for a familiar face, but I found none. The next day passed exactly the same way. And the next. Then, on my third day of walking around aimlessly, I found my friend Yitzik, one of the shoemakers at Annaburg. I hadn't seen Yitzik since we walked into the showers shortly after our arrival at Gross-Rosen.

"Join me for a walk, Kalman," he said. "This place is awful. But I heard that if you volunteer to get the soup pots from the kitchen, you pass by the women's camp. Maybe we will be able to see our wives if we head that way. I told the kapo with the wooden bat that I would bring the soup. You'll help me."

We walked through the men's camp, which was full of prisoners sitting on the frozen ground. There were a few men walking around, most of whom I assumed were recent arrivals like us, still able to walk. When we neared the women's camp, I heard a familiar voice.

"Yitzik! Yitzik!"

It was Genia.

"Yitzik, where's Kalman?" she continued.

"I'm here, it's me," I said as we got closer.

"I did not recognize you," Genia told me through the fence.

It had been only a few days since we last saw each other and I was unrecognizable. We had to be brief. This was not Annaburg; the guards at Gross-Rosen would not take kindly to our fraternizing with the female inmates.

"Just stay alive, Genia. Please do all that you can to stay alive," I told her as Yitzik and I continued on to the kitchen to bring the soup.

We carried the pot back towards the men's camp, straight to the kapo with the bat, careful not to drop it. It was a pot of dirty water that they called soup. No wonder everyone here was so weak and sick. We were all literally starving.

Yitzik and I volunteered to get the soup every day of the six weeks we spent in Gross- Rosen. But we did not see our wives again. I did not know if Genia was still at Gross-Rosen or even still alive, and I had no way of finding out. At least I had Yitzik. We spent all our time together, walking outside to stay strong when the weather allowed, and sleeping near each other in the barrack.

In February of 1945, Gross-Rosen was evacuated. The Russians were getting close, but not close enough. I was stuffed into an overcrowded cattle car and sent to Buchenwald. I lost Yitzik in the chaos of boarding the train and I never saw him again.

CHAPTER 21

W E ARRIVED AT Buchenwald at night, blinded by floodlights as we exited the train. The yelling was back. It began immediately.

"Out! Out! Jews! Line up with your backs to the train! Backs to the train!"

There were no women on our train, so no need to separate the men from the women. I found a place in line and for the first time ever, struggled to stand. My knees felt like they would buckle at any moment. I had watched so many men just drop in place at Gross-Rosen and had prided myself on keeping up my strength. Now, after just six weeks at Gross-Rosen and a freezing train ride, I was so frightened to feel unsteady on my feet. I willed myself to hold my head up straight and hoped that my legs would not fail me.

Luckily, we were a small group, and the line of men quickly began moving toward Buchenwald's main gate. There were no showers, which meant that we were not being gassed, but also that we would remain dirty and lice-ridden. I was relieved to feel my legs steadying as I walked, and hopeful that the instability I had felt just a few minutes ago was stiffness from the train, rather than frailty.

We walked through the main gate straight to Buchenwald's "little camp," where the kapos assigned us numbers. I waited my turn on line until I reached a square table with four chairs, which struck me as unusual. The only tables I had seen in concentration camps up to that point were long, rectangular tables. There were no Nazis in sight. Two kapos dressed in striped uniforms sat at the table, a stack of cards and an open notebook in front of them. I looked down at the open page on the notebook and saw the date. I had arrived at Buchenwald on February 10, 1945.

There were two empty chairs at the table, but they did not offer me a seat, so I stood as they asked me basic questions: name, date of birth, place of birth, and what they called "last location." I answered their questions, listing Gross-Rosen as my "last location," and they told me my number.

"One – two – eight – three – five – three," one of them said.

"Remember that number," said the other, "it is your new name."

"One – two – eight – three – five – three," I repeated under my breath, as I followed the line of men in front of me.

I was exhausted, but I knew I had to memorize that number. I said it over and over again in my head as I walked. I would never forget those six digits.

"One – two – eight – three – five – three, one – two – eight – three – five – three, one – two – eight – three – five – three...."

Separated from the main camp by a barbed wire fence, the little camp was where all newcomers arrived at Buchenwald. I later learned that in the earlier war years, Jews were not mixed with other prisoners at Buchenwald. By the time I arrived, however, the little camp housed Jews along with prisoners of all religions and nationalities. We all shared a miserable existence. We slept on the same four-story bunks, shared with a crowd of sick men, in windowless horse stables. There must have been over a thousand men in my stable. The sign outside said Block 58.

Like Gross-Rosen, there was no work, dirty water for soup, and nothing to do but think. Luckily, it was unseasonably warm in February of 1945, and I spent as much time as possible walking around outside. It was better than being inside the sickness-infested stables, and the sunshine and movement helped me keep up what little strength I had.

One morning, less than a week after my arrival, a kapo I did not recognize appeared at the door to the stable. He looked relatively clean and wore a striped uniform. It was the first uniform I saw since I was assigned my identification number. He stood at the entrance, avoiding actually entering the stable, which I totally understood. I would not have stepped inside if I had the choice.

"I will read several numbers from the list in front of me," he said loudly. "If you hear your number, please join me here at the entrance to your barrack."

"One – two – eight – three – five – three."

Mine was the last number he called. I did not know whether having my number called was a good thing or a bad thing, but I walked toward him behind the other three men.

"You are a Jew," he said, as I approached. He spoke German with a familiar accent.

"Yes."

"I'm sorry. I was going to take you to work, but you cannot work if you are a Jew."

"Where are you from?"

"Dabrowa."

I did recognize the accent. Dabrowa was just a few kilometers from Sosnowiec.

"I'm from Sosnowiec. Please. You can help me. I want so much to live. Just take me to work. I am stronger than almost every man here. I will work hard. I beg you."

"It's not that simple. I can't just take a Jew to work."

"Maybe you forgot to ask me if I'm Jewish."

He turned and walked away, leaving me standing alone. I watched the three other men leave, green with envy. A few years ago, I would have smiled at those men and wished them luck as they walked out of the stables, through the fence, and away from the little camp. I did not wish evil upon them, but the war had changed me. I was so jealous. I wanted out so badly it hurt. It was the closest I got to losing hope during the war. It seemed there was no way out of this little camp save death. As a Jew, I was condemned to die at Buchenwald.

That day passed like the ones before. I walked around aimlessly until sundown and then joined the others in the stable.

The next morning, the same man appeared at the doorway. He began calling out numbers, but I did not listen, knowing that he would not call mine.

Suddenly, the barrack was silent. I looked toward the kapo. He stood with three men, presumably those whose numbers I did not hear being called.

"I am calling this number for the last time," he said, breaking the silence. "One – two – eight – three – five – three."

I could not believe my ears. I jumped up, my legs moving faster than they had in months and ran to reach the barrack entrance. The kapo looked at me straight in the eye.

"You are no longer a Jew. Follow the other three men, comrade."

We followed him through the gate out of the little camp. We were given soap, uniforms, and shoes, and told to shower and change. It was the first shower I had in weeks, and it felt good to be clean. The uniform was warmer than anything I had worn since I left Annaburg. It had a red triangle on the chest, marking me as a political prisoner. I later learned that Jews at Buchenwald who were lucky enough to have uniforms wore yellow triangles.

The kapo who saved my life that morning handed each of us a piece of bread. I thanked him for the bread and never saw him again. I was on my own as a political prisoner.

The four of us walked together, each carrying a small bundle consisting of the clothing and shoes we put on when arrived, as well as our bar of soap, to an office at Block 21 to register.

"Name," said the prisoner sitting in front of a typewriter, with a Polish accent.

"Karl Sztajer." Kalman would have given me away as a Jew.

He looked up.

"I don't know a Karl Sztajer, but I recognize you. You are a Berlinsky. It's your eyes. Strong genes."

Berlinsky was my mother's maiden name. I had lasted just minutes as a non-Jew.

"I'm Zenig's son."

Zenig was my uncle's best friend. It was unusual for a religious Jew and a Pole to be close friends in Sosnowiec, but they met playing table tennis as teenagers at the local club and the friendship stuck.

"I don't know what you're doing in this part of the camp," he said, "and I don't want to know. You don't know me, and I don't know you. I will fill out your information and then you will be on your way. Stay away from me."

He proceeded to ask me a series of questions and write the answers on a large identification card.

"State your name."

"Karl Sztajer."

"Date of birth."

"December 24, 1920.

"Place of birth"

"Sosnowiec, Poland."

"Last address"

"Gross-Rosen."

"Your identification number at Gross-Rosen?"

"Nine – five – seven – seven – seven."

"And your number here at Buchenwald?"

"One – two – eight – three – five – three."

"Occupation?"

"Carpenter."

"That's all," he said, as he placed the card on top of a pile of completed cards.

Then, he turned to the next guy in line and I followed the prisoner in front of me down a long hallway where we joined a line of prisoners dressed in uniforms. I considered myself lucky to be standing there, no matter how long the line; I was out of the little camp, standing inside a warm building, wearing clean clothing, and holding a piece of bread in my pocket. I reached the front of the line after a few hours and was shocked to see a sign on the door.

"Medical Office."

"Next," I heard, as the door opened in front of me.

I entered what looked like an actual doctor's office. Standing on the other side of the door was a portly man in a white coat holding a clipboard. I could not remember the last time I saw a doctor, or anyone overweight; prisoners were all emaciated and while they must have existed, I had not seen a heavyset Nazi soldier.

"Prisoner number," he said.

"One – two – eight – three – five – three."

The doctor looked down at the clipboard in his hand and read my number aloud. He motioned for me to sit on the table and examined me as though I was there for a routine physical examination. He looked into my throat, listened to my heart, checked my pulse, and measured my height. He did not check my weight. Aside from the sound of my own voice reading letters off the eye chart on the wall, the exam took place in silence.

"You are fit to work," the doctor said, speaking for the first time since he asked for my prisoner number.

I watched him underline my prisoner number on his clipboard, literally saving my life with a stroke of his pen. I stood taller as he opened the door for me to step back into the hallway. I was going to work! I was clean! I was out of the little camp! Things were looking up for me at that moment.

A prisoner in a striped uniform with a green triangle on it directed me outside and into another building, marked Wing D. There, I waited on yet another line for my turn to see the Nazi officer in charge of this area in the camp.

"You're a Jew," he said, as I walked in the room. Do I have a sign on my head or something? I thought.

"That's none of your business," I told him, trying to sound tough. I was actually terrified. "Just be sure nothing happens to me on your watch. If I'm hurt or I disappear, you have five minutes to get lost before you're dead. They will find you."

I said the last sentence really slowly, like I meant it, like he had real reason to be afraid.

"You'll find the labor office just down the hall to your left," he told me, his eyes wide open. I had scared him. He was in shock. So was I. What had become of me?

I made my way down the hall like nothing unusual had happened. He must have thought I was a communist. The communist prisoners exerted a lot of control at Buchenwald. They had a certain independence that the other prisoners lacked. They were able to move around freely, and controlled the labor office, where they assigned work to prisoners. Many of the Nazi guards were afraid to tangle with the political prisoners, mostly communists.

Most importantly for my purpose – survival – the political prisoners were treated nothing like Jews. I answered the same questions I had just a few minutes earlier, and the communist sitting behind the desk at the labor office filled in yet another card with my information. This time, I elaborated a bit about my carpentry experience, and he assigned me the temporary job of "fix-it man" around the offices and barracks. I would get a permanent assignment soon, he said.

As a political prisoner, my world was so very different from the one I left at the little camp. I felt a mixture of happiness and guilt. I was clean, wore a uniform, slept in my own bunk, and would receive Red Cross packages. Each Red Cross package was meant to be shared among six to eight political prisoners, and contained socks, chocolates, and cigarettes.

I had only been labeled a political prisoner for three days when I received my share of the first box. I immediately put the socks on over the ones already on my feet. It made my shoes a bit tight, but even political prisoners were cold in Buchenwald in the winter. I put the chocolate and cigarettes in my pockets and waited for the sun to set. When the sky turned a darker shade of gray and the howl of the wind began to intensify, I walked over to the little camp fence. I did not wait until the sky was completely dark because I had to be sure that if I was seen, my red triangle would be visible.

Over the last few days, I had learned just how much control the communists had in Buchenwald. One could never be one hundred percent sure of a Nazi guard's reaction, but I was fairly confident that if I walked over to the fence with purpose, any guard who saw me and my red triangle would leave me alone.

No one saw me. Or if someone did, I was not made aware. I have to assume it was my red triangle. The little camp seemed deserted as I walked toward the fence, although maybe it always looked that way; when I was in the little camp, I did not often walk around after dark. I stuck the cigarettes and the chocolate through the links in the fences and watched them drop to the ground on the other side. Then I turned around and headed back to my barrack, hoping that a prisoner in the little camp would get a hold of my chocolate and cigarettes. About halfway back, I stopped. I did not really need the extra socks. I sat on the ground in the middle of Buchenwald, removed my second pair of socks, walked back to the fence, and stuck those through too.

The following month, I dropped a new pair of socks through the fence along with the cigarettes and chocolate.

CHAPTER 22

THE RED CROSS packages stopped arriving sometime in late winter of 1945. Or at least they stopped being distributed to the prisoners. Otherwise, life continued as usual for us political prisoners. I was assigned a permanent job placement in mid-March. The communist kapo in charge of my barrack approached me while I was playing cards with another prisoner.

"Karl. You've been assigned a job."

"I already have a job. I fix everything that breaks around here."

"You are quite handy. We need your skills around our barrack and offices, but if anyone asks, you are assigned to labor detachment 97, responsible for camp enlargement. To keep the Nazis off our backs, the labor office must assign each man a permanent position. Nothing will change for you."

"Alright," I told him. "I'm part of labor detachment 97."

He walked away, and I laughed along with my card-playing barrack mate. We knew that there was no enlargement taking place at Buchenwald. The Nazis were not in a position to expand anything. Some of the communist prisoners had access to a radio and by early spring it seemed clear from the broadcasts that the Americans were not far from Buchenwald.

One day in early April, the Americans dropped three empty drums in the middle of the camp. It was a signal to both the Nazis and the prisoners – the Americans were close. It was the last day we received our daily food rations and the last day we went to work.

The following afternoon, an announcement was made on the camp loudspeakers that all Jews were to congregate for roll call. I had been living as a non-Jew in Buchenwald and could not expose myself as a Jew. I decided not to go. I would be shot.

For reasons unknown to me, the roll call was postponed to the next day and was expanded to include all prisoners. Everyone, even political prisoners, was to be at roll call the following morning, according to the announcement.

Another night of uncertainty passed. I did not sleep. I was both excited at the prospect of the war's ending – at having survived – and also terrified that I would not survive, that I would be found out as a Jew at the roll call and killed so close to the end.

The next morning, the entire group of political prisoners in my wing stayed back from the roll call. A Nazi officer arrived at the entrance to our barrack.

"We are looking for Jews," he said. "We know there are Jews hiding throughout the camp."

"There are no Jews here. Only political prisoners," the kapo told him.

"All of you get to the roll call now," said the Nazi. "If we find a Jew hidden among you, we will kill the whole block. You have fifteen minutes before we come back with guns. Whoever is not at roll call will be shot. Fifteen minutes."

None of the prisoners gave me up. I worried that some, if not all of them, likely knew that I was Jewish. But no one said a word. Three men walked out of the barrack after a few minutes, presumably on their way to the roll call, but most of us did not leave the barrack. I felt the others' eyes on me as I walked to my bunk. Of course, they knew I was a Jew.

I knew what to do. Layering saves lives in concentration camps. I took off my uniform and dressed in the ill-fitting clothing I wore when I arrived at Buchenwald. Then, I put the uniform back on, over that clothing. I sat on my bunk and waited.

As expected, fifteen minutes later, the guards charged straight into the barracks with guns blazing. They shot at everything that moved. There was nothing to do but run and hope to avoid bullets. So I ran, as quickly as I could, all the way out of the barracks and to the main entrance of Buchenwald.

When I arrived at the gates, I saw what looked like a few hundred inmates being marched out of Buchenwald. None of the prisoners on this particular march were Jewish, or at least none were identifiable as Jews based on yellow triangles or old rags for clothes. Everyone marching wore a uniform with a red, green, or blue triangle.[13] At the time, another march seemed like a better idea than being shot at, so I joined the masses. At least it wasn't as cold as it was the last time I was on a march.

This march was brief; it stopped at the train tracks nearby. I climbed into the boxcar train with the others, where I must have fallen asleep standing up, yet again.

The bombing woke me. I don't know how long I was asleep, but we had not gone far. The Americans! They had bombed the tracks in front of us. I watched the flames glow, ecstatic at the destruction of the path to wherever the Nazis wanted to take us.

The train stopped. Some of the prisoners removed their shirts, waving them in the air, presumably to let the Americans above know not to drop a bomb on us. The Nazi guards forced us off the train to begin another march. They did not yell at all. By April of 1945, the Nazis had apparently found their inside voices.

This time, the Nazis marched with us, mixed in among us, their fear of the Americans obvious. It was a good time to escape. I slowly made my way to the left side of the road where there was an embankment. I walked along the edge for a few hours, and just as the sun was beginning to set, I lay on the ground and rolled down the embankment.

I lay on the ground until dark, afraid to be seen. Despite the American planes above, the Nazis were still in charge here – in my corner of earth. The moon was just a tiny sliver that night, and the pitch black allowed me to be completely hidden. I undressed, and redressed, this time with my prisoner's uniform covered by my ill-fitting clothing. I walked to the nearest home, just a few minutes from the embankment. I drank some water from a small brook just outside the house, and let myself into the barn, hoping I could rest

---

13. Criminals were identified by green triangles. Forced foreign laborers were identified by blue triangles.

overnight and figure out where to go next. Fortunately, the barn was empty and even had a sleeping loft. I climbed up and fell asleep as soon as I put my head down.

The sun woke me, peeking through the barn's slatted walls, and my first thought was food. I did not remember the last time I had eaten. I lifted my head, the first step toward making my way outside to the brook for some water, and heard people talking outside. My roofing experience came in handy as I silently removed a small shingle above the sleeping loft. I looked out the hole to find a group of men dressed in Buchenwald prisoner uniforms sitting on the ground eating what looked like a picnic. They held long loaves of bread and drank out of ceramic mugs. Maybe it was coffee, was all I could think, as I swapped my clothing once again, and walked out of the barn towards them in my political prisoner uniform.

A woman approached me on my way.

"What were you doing in my barn?" she asked.

"I was passing by last night and was overwhelmed by exhaustion. I slept in your barn and just woke to hear my fellow prisoners."

I was too tired to come up with a lie, and I am not even sure what else I could have said to improve my situation. The truth seemed like as good a story as any to this woman whose barn I had used without her permission.

"You've been liberated," she said. "The Americans have taken over Buchenwald. Go join the other men eating on the grass, please. There is enough for all of you. I hope that wherever they are, someone is feeding my husband and son."

That was how I heard about the liberation. Alone. For years, I waited for the Nazis to fall, to fail, to lose the war. And when they finally did, I was without family, without friends, without a single other Jew to share my joy.

Still, I felt a smile forming on my face. It started small, my lips curling up only slightly on both sides of my mouth. By the time I walked over to the group of men sitting on the ground, I had a huge grin on my face. I had done it! I had survived!

I sat down with the other men, ate some bread, and drank a cup of tea. Turns out, the coffee I was hoping for was just a dream. I introduced myself as Karl, a political prisoner. As happy as I was to have heard that the Americans liberated Buchenwald, there was no reason to take any chances. I did not know these men; they may not have been pleased to break bread with a Jew. I hoped I wasn't the only one who survived. Was I the last Jew in Europe? I thought to myself as I stood up and walked up the embankment and onto the road.

CHAPTER 23

T HE ROAD WAS deserted, not a single person in sight. I stood alone with no idea where to go, no idea which direction to choose. But I had to go somewhere, so I walked left. It wasn't long before a row of American tanks appeared, just outside what I later learned was the town of Jena. I stood on the edge of the road and watched in awe as the tanks passed.

Then I followed the tanks into Jena and observed the scene. Some of the American soldiers climbed out of their tanks as German civilians filled the streets, children cheered, some even held small white flags. Watching the celebrations, you would have thought that these Germans, who lived in such close proximity to concentration camps, were themselves being liberated. I watched, unsure what to make of people who I believed shared blame for the Nazi effort now cheering its downfall.

An American soldier approached me. He stopped a couple of feet in front of me and said something in English I did not understand. When I lifted my palms in a universal "I do not understand" gesture, he handed me a small piece of paper and pencil from his chest pocket. I drew a Star of David and handed it back.

"Jude?" he asked.

I nodded in response. He knew at least one word of German.

He took the rifle off his shoulder and placed it on the ground in between us. Then he emptied his pockets into his hands and held them open in front of me. I took a few coins, a pack of cigarettes, a candy bar, and the first package of chewing gum I had ever seen. I swallowed the pieces of gum whole as he watched. At the time, I thought maybe he had never met a Jew before. I did not realize that the confusion I saw in his face was over my swallowing twelve sticks of chewing gum as though they were food.

He motioned for me to follow him, and I did. He escorted me into a bakery, walked behind the counter, took a small loaf of bread, and handed it to me, while the man I assumed was the proprietor stood by without saying a word. The chewing gum did not agree with my stomach, so I decided to wait to eat the bread. I held on to that bread tightly, saving it for later; I had been hungry too much over the last few years to take any food for granted. I followed him down the street and into the middle of a group of American soldiers. Most of them were close to my age but looked so young and healthy, with full cheeks, in contrast to my own hollow face.

The soldiers stopped talking as soon as I stood among them. My escort smiled at me and turned to talk to an older soldier who I assumed was an officer. The officer reached out his hand and shook mine, then spoke to a short skinny soldier on his right – who looked no older than fifteen – in rapid English I could not decipher.

"Come with us," said the short man in German. "I am a translator with the American army. My grandparents were German and did not learn English after they immigrated to the United States, so I grew up speaking German to them. My officer asks that you join him at the new Army Headquarters."

"Yes, I will join him," I answered.

An American Army Headquarters? Of course I would join him. I had nowhere else to be and no idea where else to go.

As we walked through the streets of Jena, I told the translator a very abbreviated version of where I had been during the war and learned that I was not the only Jew who survived.

"You should go back to Buchenwald," he said after I told him where I had been.

"Why would I ever go back to Buchenwald? I never want to see that place again."

"But that's where your people are."

"My people? I told you that I am not really a communist. I just got this uniform because I lied about who I am. Those political prisoners are not my people. I am a Jew."

"Yes. Your people. The Jews. The Jews are at Buchenwald!"

"The Jews are dead," I told him, fairly certain I was the only European Jew alive.

"Some Jews at Buchenwald are alive. Too many of them are close to death, but there are living Jews at Buchenwald. Jews who survived the camp. I'll ask my commander if we can take you there when we're done at headquarters. You'll see for yourself."

I had assumed all the Jews left at Buchenwald had been starved, shot, or marched to death. I was shocked. Suddenly, I could not wait to get back to Buchenwald.

I followed the Americans into a building they were using as temporary offices. After another discussion in English I could not understand, we entered a small room with a table in the center. On one side, sat an American soldier holding a pen, a black notebook open on the table in front of him. Two men in Gestapo uniforms sat on the other side.

"Prisoners," the translator began. Instinctively, I jumped. I realized he wasn't talking to me when the Gestapo soldiers stood.

"Empty your bags," he continued, as he put his arm around my shoulder.

"This is my friend Karl. He is going to take whatever he wants from your bags."

The American soldier who had been sitting when I entered the room stood up and handed me a green canvas backpack. I watched the Nazis pile their belongings onto the table and then I silently filled my new bag with all of the food they placed there. I also took a pen and a small screwdriver. I left the clothing. I did not want to see any part of a Nazi uniform ever again.

I turned to the translator.

"Can we go to Buchenwald now?"

CHAPTER 24

BUCHENWALD LOOKED VERY much the same as it had when I left. The camp was in the process of being cleaned up, and survivors were receiving medical care after years of malnutrition and illness. Some of those providing the care were themselves former inmates, doctors, and nurses who had suffered with their patients, but now took on the responsibility of healing. I registered with a committee that had been set up for the purposes of identifying and helping survivors.

The American army chaplain, Rabbi Schachter from New York, posted daily lists of survivors found at other camps around Europe. I spent hours alongside fellow survivors, poring over lists for familiar names. After three days of searching, I finally found Genia's name.

She was alive!

The list was titled *Survivors of Bergen Belsen*. I had not known she was there. I had to get there as soon as possible.

I ran as quickly as I could to the Rabbi's office. There was a line outside and I had no choice but to wait. Full of nervous energy, I walked around in circles, bouncing on my toes the whole time, like a small child who could not sit still at school.

"Rabbi," I said, as soon as it was my turn to enter his office. "My wife is on the list! She is on the list! My wife is alive in Bergen Belsen! I need to get to Bergen Belsen. Can you take me?"

The words flew out of my mouth as quickly as I thought them. I could not slow them down and I felt out of breath as I spoke.

"I cannot leave here. I am so sorry."

"How will I get to her?" I asked, struggling to catch my breath.

"I will figure something out," he said. "Go to the Office for the Committee for Passports this afternoon to get the appropriate travel documents. Then come see me first thing in the morning."

Like the other Jewish survivors at Buchenwald, I had no identification at all, and I could not go to Bergen Belsen without it. Both the Americans and the British required anyone traveling in areas under their control to have identification, and the Americans established a committee at Buchenwald to provide survivors with the necessary documents.

I found my way to the passport office and was shocked to see the long line outside. It was longer than the one outside the Rabbi's office. As soon as I found my place at the end, a man approached and told me in German that they were not taking any more applications that day. He was not an American, but appeared to be a former inmate who was working for the committee. I would have to come back tomorrow.

"Please. I just found out that my wife is alive. I need these papers to go find her. There must be something you can do."

"I'm sorry. The office will close in two hours and there is no way we will get to you today. The man in front of you is the last one who will get his papers today."

"Please, I beg you. I need the papers today. I'll just stand here and maybe the line will move more quickly than you think. There's no harm in waiting."

He shrugged and walked away.

I waited as the line inched up slowly in front of me. I had plenty of time to practice in my head exactly what I would say if they tried to close the office before I got my papers. There were a handful of people in front of me when my rehearsal was interrupted by a familiar voice behind me.

"Karl Sztajer."

"Excuse me," I said, as I turned to see who was calling my fake name. No one had called me Karl since the American translator said goodbye a few days ago.

"Karl, what are you doing here?" It was Roman. He was a political prisoner housed in my wing when I was Karl.

"I am not Karl. I am Kalman. I am a Jew."

"A Jew," he smirked and shook his head. "We all thought you were a bigwig communist under the protection of the Polish communist party. We thought the Nazis couldn't touch you. You're just a Jew? Unbelievable. You fooled us all. What are you doing at the documentation office?"

"I pretended that I was not Jewish in order to survive Buchenwald, and I am here to get identification for travel. Today, I found out that my wife is alive. I would like to leave here as soon as possible to find her. I'm waiting, hoping that when I get to the front of this line, someone in the office will take pity on me and give me documents before the office closes."

"We will give you the documents. I'm on the committee. I am just heading back to the office from a meeting with the Americans. I'll be sure we stay open until you have what you need."

And they did. I received a card with my name, date, and place of birth. I was to have it with me at all times, much like the documentation the Nazis provided at the beginning of the war. This one was meant to protect me though, not condemn me.

I walked back to the barrack too excited to sleep. I sat upright all night. I walked over to Rabbi Schachter's office before dawn, hoping to be first on the line outside his office when he arrived. I was surprised to see him already seated at his desk, his door open. He looked up when I arrived and waved me inside.

"Good morning, Rabbi. I'm not sure if you remember me," I began as I walked into the room, ready to explain why I came to see him.

"Of course I remember you. You were here yesterday. You're the young man whose wife was found alive in Bergen Belsen. You need a way to get there. As of now, the next truck heading in that direction isn't leaving here for a few days."

"I can't wait a few days. I will go crazy just sitting here and waiting. What if she is sick? So many of us are. How do I know she will even be there when I arrive? And what if she leaves before I get there? Survivors are traveling all over Europe looking for family and friends. Please, help me. I hope I can find her, but I am helpless."

I was out of breath again.

"I will do my best to help you," he continued, as he handed me a piece of paper and a pen.

"Write a note to your wife letting her know that you will meet her at Bergen Belsen. I will have your note sent to your wife today so that she knows to wait for you there. Then, you will take my bicycle and ride to find your wife."

"Your bicycle?"

"Yes. The army gave me a bicycle. If it becomes necessary for me to travel, I have other means of transportation at my disposal. The soldier standing outside my office will show you the bicycle. And keep this letter with your identification. It says that you are borrowing my personal bicycle. You do not want to be caught with a U.S. Army bicycle without permission."

"Thank you."

We stood and shook hands. We both knew he wasn't getting the bicycle back. I handed him the note I had scribbled to Genia.

Genia, I am alive. I am on my way to you. Do not leave Bergen Belsen. I will be there as soon as I can, Kalman.

CHAPTER 25

T HE BICYCLE WAS army green, like my new backpack, with a brown saddle. The soldier outside the Rabbi's office walked over to the bike with me, demonstrated how to attach the small tool bag to the saddle, and handed me a map indicating the way to Bergen Belsen. We could not communicate, but he smiled as he handed me a pack of chewing gum, and I was on my way.

I rode the bike back to the barracks to retrieve my backpack. I was shaky at first, but whoever said you don't forget how to ride a bike knew what he was talking about. I quickly adjusted to riding, collected my backpack full of food, said goodbye to the men I had met over the last few days, and rode out of Buchenwald's main gate.

The ride to Bergen Belsen, almost three hundred kilometers, took me almost a week. I struggled along the way. While I was stronger than many survivors, I was still weak and malnourished. The first day was especially slow going. I hadn't slept the night before and my legs simply did not have enough strength to take me very far. I rode as far as I could before stopping. I spent that night, and several that followed, asleep on the side of the road, the Rabbi's bicycle at my side.

I developed a routine as I rode. I woke up each morning and biked until my legs burned, at which point I took a break and had something to eat. At first, my breaks were frequent and rather lengthy, but as I gained strength, I was able to ride for longer periods of time. I slowly made my way through the food I got from the Gestapo bags at Jena. After a snack and a break, I would ride again, as far as my legs would take me, until I was done for the day.

I encountered all sorts of people along the way, mostly survivors, Jews heading back to their homes, looking for lost loved ones. I stayed away from anyone who did not look like a survivor – we had a distinct appearance – or an American or British soldier. Somewhere along the way, the American soldiers were replaced by British ones. Aside from their uniforms, they were no different. They left me alone as I passed, smiled and waved, and sometimes offered food using the few German words they knew.

When I arrived at Bergen Belsen, I stepped off the bike and walked through the main entrance to the camp. There was a group of women sitting peeling potatoes a few feet to my left.

"Do any of you know Genia Sztajer?" I asked in German.

None of them even looked up at me. I moved on to the next group of women, and the next. I walked around for what felt like hours asking every single woman I saw, "Do you know Genia Sztajer?"

Finally, one woman spoke up.

"You're looking for Genia? Genia Sztajer?"

"Yes."

"You must be her husband." She grabbed her head with both hands and fell to her knees.

"Creator of the Universe," she cried, tears streaming down her cheeks. "God sent me here. I am an angel sent to this awful place for a reason. I am going to reunite a couple that lived through the war. They will be together again."

I stood by silently as this stranger sat on the ground and cried. I looked around as others approached, and before I knew it, I was standing in the middle of a group of almost fifty women, several more of them crying now. I was getting impatient. I leaned down and spoke to the stranger who knew Genia.

"Please, can you show me where to find my wife?" I asked gently.

She stood and as we walked, followed by the crowd, through Bergen Belsen, I imagined myself watching the scene from above. It looked more like a funeral procession than a reunion, except for the man in front. A group of sad-looking, emaciated, mostly bald people followed a crying woman who walked shoulder to shoulder with a smiling young man. When they reached the end of a dirt path, the crying woman stopped and pointed to a door. The man nodded at her and tapped on the door, his smile widening as his own eyes filled with tears.

"It's me," I heard.

AFTERWORD

K ALMAN AND GENIA arrived at the Feldafing displaced persons camp shortly after their reunion. They weighed their postwar immigration options – Palestine or the United States – until Kalman found his second cousin, Arthur Numberg, among the survivors at Feldafing. Arthur, a once-active member of the Polish Bund, had been promised passage to New York in exchange for a commitment to continue his socialist activism on behalf of the Bund in New York. Arthur arranged for Kalman and Genia to join Arthur and his wife, and the group of four arrived in New York on May 24, 1946.

Kalman's maternal aunt and her family, the Marks, took in the young couple and shared exciting news; Sol, Max, Henry, and Julia all survived the war and were living in Paris. Sadly, they also confirmed that the couple's parents, along with Henry and Aaron, had been sent to the gas chambers immediately upon arrival at Auschwitz in 1943.

As Kalman and Genia slowly rebuilt their lives and moved into their own apartment on Rivington Street in the Lower East Side, they put aside money each month for passage to Paris and for a house where they could raise a family. Three years after they arrived in New York, Genia left Kalman in their new Brooklyn home and spent several weeks in Paris.

In 1954, they moved with their two young children, Neil and Sherry, to Danielson, Connecticut, where they joined a community of Holocaust survivors raising families in the area. Kalman built a chicken farm and the couple worked the farm together, along with their children. Tragically, eleven-year-old Neil was killed by a drunk driver while waiting for the school bus in September, 1962. Once again, the couple struggled against adversity and moved forward. They lived and worked on the farm until 1980, when they moved to New York City to be closer to their grandchildren.

Kalman passed away on February 13, 2007. He was survived by Genia, Sherry, three grandchildren and nine great-grandchildren. After Kalman's death, Genia was blessed with three more great-grandsons, all of whom share his name.

Shlomo Berlinsky, Kalman's maternal
grandfather. United States Holocaust
Memorial Museum Collection

Nachum and Leah Sztajer, Kalman's parents
(undated). United States Holocaust Memorial
Museum Collection

Sztajer family (1932). Nachum, Aaron, Julia, Kalman, Herschel, and Leah (left to right). United States Holocaust Memorial Museum Collection

Unknown group (Summer 1937). Max Eckstein (top left), Sol Eckstein (second from left, top), Henry Eckstein (top right), Genia Eckstein (second from right, middle). United States Holocaust Memorial Museum Collection

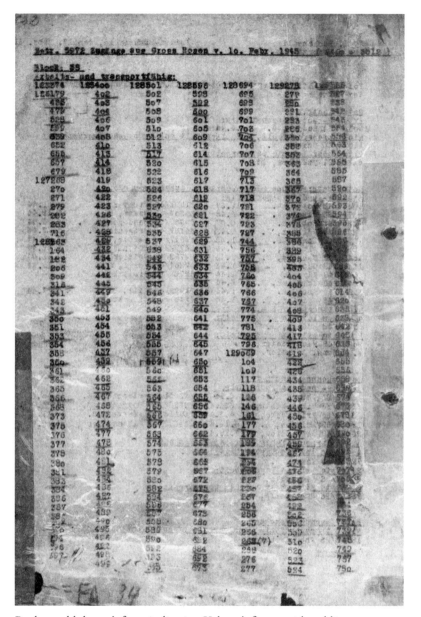

Buchenwald doctor's form indicating Kalman's fitness with red line.
Arolsen Archives

Kalman's Buchenwald *Facharbeiterkarte* (skilled
worker card), identifying him as a *Zimmerer*
(carpenter), working at the labor detachment
Lagererweiterung (camp enlargement).
Arolsen Archives

Kalman's Buchenwald *Zugangsbogen*, prisoner registration form.
Arolsen Archives

Genia's Feldafing Displaced Persons Index Card (1945).
United States Holocaust Memorial Museum Collection

Arthur Numberg, Kalman's cousin (undated).
United States Holocaust Memorial Museum Collection

Kalman and Genia, New York, New York (1946).
United States Holocaust Memorial Museum Collection